DUANE ERROL FLEMING

Building a New America with
CHRIST'S VALUES

How to Create Good, Sustainable Jobs and Shift to
Renewable Energy Before Oil is Unaffordable

WESTBOW®
PRESS
A DIVISION OF THOMAS NELSON
& ZONDERVAN

WestBow Press books may be ordered through booksellers or by contacting:

WestBow Press
A Division of Thomas Nelson & Zondervan
1663 Liberty Drive
Bloomington, IN 47403
www.westbowpress.com
1 (866) 928-1240

ISBN: 978-1-4908-4168-7 (sc)
ISBN: 978-1-4908-4170-0 (hc)
ISBN: 978-1-4908-4169-4 (e)

Library of Congress Control Number: 2014911297

Printed in the United States of America.

WestBow Press rev. date: 7/21/2014

CONTENTS

PREFACE

I have written *Building a New America with Christ's Values* because America is a nation in need of solutions to problems that can no longer be ignored. There is an urgent need to design and implement new job creation systems to employ the vast army of the unemployed and the underemployed. For over 30 years, I have followed the wonderful progress of the Mondragon Cooperative Corporation, which now provides the foundation for creating good, sustainable jobs within a community that has taken control of their lives. Mondragon was founded by a Catholic priest based on the values that Christ taught of Truth, Goodness, Justice and pursuit of the Common Good with love. It is not socialism, communism, or capitalism. Mondragon is based on the principles of Christ's values.

I am inspired by Pope Francis, a pope who has defined many of the major flaws in the current economic system. He has written in *Joy of the Gospel,* "No to a financial system that rules rather than serves."

The "deified market" is destroying our global environment by burning fossil fuels, which is causing catastrophic climate disasters, killing hundreds of thousands around the world. As an urban planner, I have had the opportunity and joy of researching economics, new town planning, transportation, energy and the pursuit of the common good.

Building a New America with Christ's Values also describes a report by the Department of Defense (DOD) that America must be independent of oil by 2040. The DOD declared that it cannot guarantee affordability or availability of oil 30 years hence. The solution is to switch to the lowest cost energy, which is now solar, wind and hydrogen when we use full cost accounting.

Pope Francis also inspires because he leads with hope and joy. I trust that you will find hope and joy as you read about the available solutions. I wish to thank a member of the Board of the Livelihood Systems Institute, Merle Funkhouser, for his support and counsel. Professor Martha Thie, Terry Reed and my daughter Heidi Fleming-Alexander have given me full-hearted encouragement along the way.

Finally, I wish to thank everyone that I have quoted in this work, for I have entered into their labors. Their voices are now joined together in one book to advance all of their fine insights and work. You may find video presentations as excerpts from this book on our website, livelihoodsystems.com

INTRODUCTION

This book focuses on three powerful driving forces at work on a global scale today. These interlocking forces require solutions that are also interlocking, as follows.

(1) the need to supply sustainable livelihoods with a new Christian job creation system;

(2) the need to shift to renewable energy before oil becomes unaffordable and/or unavailable; and

(3) the need to rapidly eliminate carbon dioxide and methane to reduce global warming and super destructive climate change.

To create enough good jobs for people to make a living, we will need to establish corporations with Christian values of Truth, Justice, Sharing and Cooperation. Pope Francis has laid bare some of the many flaws of the capitalist economic structure. In his Apostolic Exhortation, *Joy of the Gospel,* the pope writes: "No to a financial system which rules rather than serves."[1] Under globalization, humankind is forced to compete under a new tyranny that does not provide enough livelihoods. Clearly, any economic system worth its salt must serve the needs of humankind.

The Creator has given humankind a precious oil supply until we could develop new energies to replace oil. Wind and solar are now the lowest cost energies, when we use full cost accounting. Wind costs 7 cents per KWH and solar cells cost about 13 cents per KWH, while the national residential average was 12 cents per KWH in 2013, according to the U.S. Energy Information Agency. It is time to make the shift to renewables because we reached Peak Oil in 2006, according to the International Energy Agency which reported that 75% of the "easy to get" oil will be gone in just 25 years. We cannot afford to run out of oil and have total economic system collapse.

Burning fossil fuels is creating climate change at an unprecedented rate. In order to save Planet Earth and our children from catastrophic disasters, we must be good stewards and help each other as Christ has taught us. Pope Francis wrote: "In this system, which tends to devour everything that stands in the way of increased profits, whatever is fragile, like the environment is defenseless before the interests of the deified market, become(s) the only rule."[2]

The long-range planning deadline for real solutions to these problems has already come and gone. The time for action is now. As we will see, delay is not an option with regard to fossil fuel burning. Scientific advancements have been made to replace fossil fuels with renewable energies. Renewable energies are no longer "alternative" energies," they are the lowest cost energies. Also, major car manufacturers are choosing hydrogen fuel cell cars over electric battery cars.

The world will be forced to deal with those issues as many leaders realize that the Age of Oil is over. The threat of ever rising gasoline prices will force the politicians out of their lethargy, but to date, far too slowly. Again, delay is not an option. The changes that we need to make will require a return to Christ's teachings and values. We can no longer live on Planet Earth by using self-interest, greed and the rape of Nature as our destructive operating procedures. Warring and insisting on Democracy at the point of a gun has nearly bankrupt America. Christ taught us "As I have loved you, love one another." (John 13:35). It is time to act with love. We have tried "business as usual" with false values and we need to realize that it has failed.

The first solution is to put in place new economic arrangements that supply decent paying jobs that are sustainable "livelihood systems", i.e., good, secure jobs with the capability of providing for family life, owning a home, education, and a comfortable retirement. There is a highly successful economic model that has done this for 50 years, as we shall see. The major reason that Americans accept capitalism, with all of its inequalities and lack of justice is because they have never been presented with a viable alternative. Fortunately, new economic arrangements in the form of worker/owner cooperatives can now provide an excellent alternative. The Mondragon Cooperative Corporation, is a highly successful worker/owner corporation that is based on Christian values as we shall see in Part 1.

There are an estimated 27 million, or more, Americans who are unemployed or under-employed. There are thousands of Americans who have served in the military that are coming home to a severely depressed job market. There are over 50 million young people in the Middle East and North Africa who have no employment or are underemployed and they have rebelled because they justly want a life. The World Economic Forum has determined that 40% of the world's unemployed are youth. This is the major reason why there are protests around the world. However, people are protesting to their governments when they should be protesting against the banks and the corporate boards of directors, who are not creating nearly enough jobs. According to the World Bank there are an estimated 2.5 billion people who are living on less than $2 per day. The "free enterprise" economic system cannot produce enough low paying jobs, and does not even try to create sustainable livelihoods. State run socialism and communism have also failed to provide a viable, just and sustaining economic system.

The underlying global problem of unemployment and underemployment is expressed by Jeremy Rifkin in his 1995 book, *The End of Work-The Decline of the Global Labor Force and the Dawn of the Post-Market Era*:

"The apostles and evangelists of the Information Age entertain few if any doubts about the ultimate success of the experiment at hand. They are convinced the Third Industrial Revolution will succeed in opening up more new job opportunities than it forecloses and that dramatic *increases in productivity will be matched by elevated levels of consumer demand and the opening of new global markets* to absorb the flood of new goods and services that will become available. Their faith, and for that matter their entire world view, hinges on the correctness of these two central propositions.

The critics, on the other hand, as well as a growing number of people already left at the wayside of the current, failing economic systems, are beginning to question where the new jobs are going to come from. In a world where sophisticated information and communication technologies will be able to replace more and more of the global workforce, it is unlikely that more than a fortunate few will be retrained for the relatively scarce high-tech scientific, professional, and managerial jobs made available in the emerging knowledge sector. The very notion that millions of workers displaced by the re-engineering and automation of the agricultural, manufacturing, and service sectors can be re-trained to be scientists, engineers, technicians, executives, consultants, teachers, lawyers and the like, and then somehow find the appropriate number of job openings in the very narrow high-tech sector, seems at best a pipe dream, and at worst a delusion." [3]

While corporations have made great strides in increasing efficiency and productivity per worker, they have pursued that course with the outright goal of *eliminating jobs* in order to increase profits and wealth for the rich and the top 0.01% super rich. *The corporations have no plan for how to employ the growing army of the unemployed that their economic system has created, globally.*

The demand by young people for decent jobs is strong and getting stronger as it sweeps across the Middle East, Africa and Europe and the Occupy Wall Street movement in the U.S. In the United States, millions of young people graduated from college and cannot find sustainable livelihoods. This is a colossal breakdown of the current economic system to create enough livelihoods for the nation and the world. It is not merely an "adjustment" that the current economic system can work through, as some might contend. In order to implement an alternative way of providing sustainable livelihoods so that the majority of people can have a life will require a new business model, long range planning and rapid implementation region by region. Clearly, this is a daunting task. This book is intended to provide a vision and a long range plan that is workable to meet America's pressing needs. The author has no misunderstanding about the degree of difficulty for implementation.

As we shall see, millions of jobs can be created through new economic arrangements. The economic model of "the free enterprise system" has failed to deliver and it will be replaced by a system that provides livelihoods for the majority of human beings not just the top 30%-40% percent of the intelligence curve.

Nation building at home will require a massive shift from military and "national security" spending to create millions of new peacetime jobs, especially in renewable energy from solar, wind, hydrogen fuel cell storage, a new transportation system and a new electric grid, as well as rebuilding the nation's aging infrastructure of bridges, roads, water and sewer pipes, water purification systems and desalinization of water. As we shall see, the economic structure needs to serve humankind rather than rule over us with near absolute power.

This book is also an alert to the upward rise in gasoline prices that has already begun. We will show how Sun and wind power and hydrogen fueled cars can master the rising energy cost situation with a determined long range national plan. Without a national plan, gasoline prices can rise too quickly and overwhelm the U.S. transportation system which is almost totally dependent on cheap oil. The nation and the whole world cannot allow itself to be caught in the trap of "too little too late." Throughout this book, we will present new economic arrangements that can give us happier, sustainable and more hopeful lives.

Advancing the Forward Days of Humankind

We will show that a new, overarching national priority is how to advance the forward days of humankind, including our children and grandchildren. New ways to make a good living are already in place in the world, based on the values of cooperation, real economic freedom, justice, Democracy at the workplace and the support of family and community life. These new and hopeful economic arrangements need to be expanded and enhanced to provision Americans and the world with sustenance, rather than fight like animals as if we had no intellects and good human values to lead our nations. Humankind can supply all of us by using our metaphysical intellects and wisdom for that purpose.

A model for advancing humankind's forward days economically, is already here, in our midst. It used to be one of the best kept secrets in economics. As we shall see, the highly successful Mondragon Cooperative Corporation offers one of the best models for establishing happier and more just workplaces. It will be described in Part 1, and then we will show how it can be expanded upon to be the center of a dynamic, new regional and nation-building process. The creation of enough jobs for people to earn a decent living will require new government and private sector action with long range planning. A new corporation vision and business model must be put in place if the nation is to simply employ its people.

Part 2 will describe how the oil crunch is coming and why the domestic economy must be free from oil within the next 30-40 years. Coal and oil have been providing a "precious grub stake", an energy supply safety factor, until we were wise enough to see that the Sun, wind and cellulosic biofuels are our true sources of plentiful, clean energy.

A third overarching priority is to rapidly diminish and eliminate the emission of carbon dioxide and methane by using the renewable energies to produce carbon free energy around the globe. Global warming continues to melt massive amounts of ice at a threatening pace. Robert Kunzig, in his *National Geographic* article, "WORLD WITHOUT ICE", wrote:

"56 million years ago a mysterious surge of carbon into the atmosphere sent global temperatures soaring. In a geologic eye blink life was forever changed. Earth was hot and ice free at the end of the Paleocene epoch, with sea level 220 feet higher than now." [4]

Scientists have shown that the Earth has been through this before because of too much carbon in the atmosphere. We and Mother Nature are in a race with destiny. Mother Nature has already given us severe warnings about changing the climate, with historic droughts, fires, flooding and the melting of glaciers that provided drinking water to billions of people, now drying up from increased temperature. The warming oceans are unleashing much more rainfall, awesome flooding, snow and ice storms and hurricanes, due to global warming. Carbon dioxide is increasing acidification of the world's oceans, threatening our food supply of shellfish, fish and ultimately, all life in the ocean. This is known as global warming's "evil twin".

Droughts in the corn-belt and California are already increasing food prices and 70% of the top soil is gone. Sixty percent of the nation had unusual droughts in 2012 and the Dust Bowl is threatening to return. In Oklahoma, dramatic video footage of a massive wind-swept cloud of reddish brown dirt made visibility impossible on a stretch of Interstate-35 between Oklahoma City and Kansas City. Experts have warned for years about the impact of top soil erosion caused by industrial farming practices, including the heavy use of petroleum-based fertilizers. As the old ad said, "It's not nice to mess with Mother Nature." The solution is well known: farmers need to plant winter cover crops to enrich the soil again and eliminate tilling. Again, this is simply good stewardship of Nature, instead of destroying the source of "our daily bread."

The fossil fuel juggernaut must be rapidly replaced by renewable energies and this is the challenge to all humankind on the rapidly warming planet. In order to accomplish this global task in time, it will require us to set aside our differences and stop serving only money.

Pope Francis wrote: "No to the idolatry of money. One cause of this situation is found in our relationship to money, since we calmly accept its dominion over ourselves and our societies. The current financial crisis can make us overlook the fact that it originated in a profound human crisis: the denial of the primacy of the human person! We have created new idols. The worship of the ancient golden calf (cf. Ex32:1-35) has returned in a new and ruthless guise in the idolatry of money and the dictatorship of an impersonal economy lacking a truly human purpose. The worldwide crisis affecting finance and the economy lays bare their imbalance and, above all, their lack of real concern for human beings; man is reduced to one of his needs alone: consumption."[5]

We are now being asked to work together as never before—
to cooperate and collaborate and love each other on a global
level. The world's citizens are asked to care for each other
by caring for the natural balance of the planet, and by caring
for millions of refugees from massive flooding, wild fires,
hurricanes, and tornados. Pope Francis has said: "God forgives
and we sometimes forgive, but when nature—creation—is
mistreated, nature does not forgive." Humanity is like hot metal
melting in a crucible because of the three global driving forces
as described above. These forces can bring the world to new
unifying goals and actions.

Christ's last commandment has now come to the forefront of
life on Earth: "As I have loved you, love one another." The global
race is on to love one another. When we read the signs of the
times, God and Mother Nature are giving us clear messages
that we must stop warring, and love each other while saving
the planet, which is home to all of us. Compassion for all can
lead the world to a new unifying reflection and a new level of
consciousness, embracing love for one another.

As we shall see in Parts 2 and 3, the long range planning
horizon to make the switch from fossil fuels to wind, solar power,
and hydrogen powered cars has already arrived. Americans
may be able to afford gasoline for a while longer but the nation
cannot afford to blunder backwards into a collapsing future.
We need long range planning and the commencement of rapid
implementation in this decade and continued over the next

three decades at a scale and speed that must be more dynamic than was seen during World War II. We will need millions of cars powered by green energy, and green energy powered rapid transit systems, as oil becomes too expensive for the entire United States transportation system. It will take 30 years to build the hundreds of renewable energy power plants, a new electric grid, hydrogen powered cars and rapid transit systems that will be critically needed.

Oil may be sold around the world for 45 to 75 years or more, but at what price? And to whom shall it be sold? China can outbid the United States for oil. Science and Mother Nature have told us that we must eliminate CO_2 emissions as soon as possible. People must have a livelihood system that works with justice for all. These three global "Driving Forces" have reached "the for Christ's sake line" and, combined, leave us little choice in the matter, for self-preservation, whether we have the God-given grace to care for one another globally or not.

Natural gas is not a good bridge fuel, as it has three major problems: (1) it only reduces CO_2 emissions by about 11% when compared to oil, not 50% as advertised. Natural gas may reduce carbon emissions by 50% compared to coal, but the nation needs to rapidly shift to renewable power to survive; (2) The process of "Fracking" or hydraulic fracturing, produces huge amounts of toxic, hazardous wastewater that must be kept out of the water supply, and (3) leaking unburned methane must not continue to be released into the atmosphere, by "Fracking". As pointed out by Dr. J. William Louda, professor of environmental chemistry at Florida Atlantic University, "Each molecule of methane not combusted (oxidized) to the carbon oxides has the infrared absorption ability of 25 carbon dioxide molecules. That is why a little methane escaping into the atmosphere is such a big thing, scientifically and climatically."

We are living in a rapidly changing world, where economic necessity, fast moving climate change and oil depletion are ignored by too many people in leadership roles who are working against the well-being of individuals, nations and our only home---planet Earth. To overcome the corruption of money and power-hungry egos, we need to become more cooperative, to have compassion for one another and to seek the common good and justice. Albert Nolan has said it well: "Until we transcend our egos and discover our oneness as humans, we will continue to compare and compete, to make one another suffer, to fight and to kill. We need to see that what is best for everyone is best for us too."[6]

And again, we have the technological capabilities at hand as Bertrand Russell said long ago: "It would now be technically possible to unify the world, abolish war and poverty altogether, if men desired their own happiness more than the misery of their enemies."

A New Economic Growth Model

The old economic growth model needs to be replaced by a model that lets the Sun and wind do the work. Then cooperatives and all corporations can distribute the wealth gained back to the workers-owners who created that wealth with their investment and their labor. Sustainable development would then be based on developing massive amounts of renewable energy, lateral distribution and sharing of the energy and wealth created. Growth in wealth then would no longer be based on oil and outsourcing jobs to areas of extremely low, slave wages. Growth in wealth would no longer require such a large amount of depletion of natural resources. The economy can grow at the rate that we shift to renewable energies, using Sun, wind and hydrogen power energy to drive machines and processes that create machines and assembly lines for goods. Sustainable development and sustainable job creation are also major goals necessary to save the planet, our only home. The Financial Sector of the global economic system needs to adopt the goals and objectives cited above and steer investments to these necessary and just purposes in order to advance the forward days of humankind. Pope Francis has written in *The Joy of the Gospel*: "Not to share one's wealth with the poor is to steal from them and to take away their livelihood. It is not our own goods which we hold, but theirs."

Extreme Western Individualism Has Reached New Destructive Levels

Extreme Western individualism is a way of life that took "self-fulfillment" to mean being independent, self-sufficient, having one's own money and not depending on anyone (except for sex). This has turned out to be an exercise in egoism and selfishness. This kind of blind self-centeredness has led to disaster when the loving relationships with a spouse, family and friends are considered to be of minimal importance. In other cultures this is not seen as a positive way to live, separated and isolated from the human community, while exploiting everyone and everything to achieve selfish gratification.

Robert Bellah and a team of sociologists did an extensive study of the psychosocial effects of individualism in the U.S., between 1979 and 1984.[7] The results were very negative and shocking. The effects included alienation, loneliness, lovelessness, unhappiness and the inability to maintain relationships. Instead of reaching self-fulfillment, people became self-centered and narcissistic. They had lost touch with reality, and did not realize that the ego is a very subtle trickster. The ego can seek what is good for one's false self and this leads us to chase apparent goods, rather than real goods. The ego can trick us into thinking that we are far more important and smarter than we really are. It can even lead some to believe that "I" am all that matters.

Robert Bellah said that Western individualism has brought us "to the brink of disaster." The destructive results of selfish individualism has been demonstrated clearly, in the way "business as usual" has dramatically and dangerously resulted in the global financial meltdown, which has caused the misery of billions of people with a sustained global recession. As noted above, 2.5 billion people live on less than $2 per day according to the World Bank. Many do not have a livelihood to meet their basic human needs and the needs of their family. The "free market system" has certainly not been good for those billions of people, or for millions within the United States, Asia and Europe. We are persons and we need an economic system that treats us as persons rather than as "economic objects" to be used and abused and fired by the tens of thousands at the whim of a corporation. That is a criminal act.

Our society has operated for much too long in pursuing short range perspectives. We can no longer afford too little and too late simply because the risk is the possibility of total economic system collapse, meaning lack of jobs, enough money, and food for sustainable life, resulting in millions and perhaps billions of deaths.

Even the top 2% in income would be brought down by a total economic system collapse. They could live in isolated bunkers until their deaths but most all of their means of earning wealth would be truncated or eliminated. To ignore the coming depletion of affordable oil and to ignore massive carbon emissions is to aggressively advance the extinction of the human species, and that is psychopathic.

The "free market system" has resulted in the ongoing devastation of our natural life-support systems on a global scale. Doing "business as usual" has led to our looming self-destruction from climate change, by burning fossil fuels that cause unsustainable rising global temperatures. Unless we act aggressively to change course now, this is a Death March to extinction.

The "free market system" and business as usual" are no longer cost effective. The price we have paid, and would have continued to pay, is too dear to continue to proceed that way. The future price of keeping the current economic system is unsustainable by humankind both in dollar terms and personal financial security terms, as well as the risk to life on Earth as we know it. We have, indeed, reached "the for Christ's sake line".

If we are all to survive on this planet we will have to dramatically reduce our self-centered competition and boldly create new ways to cooperate at all levels of society. We need to cooperate to survive and help other nations to survive, as they in turn will help us. The war between those who want to compete, to grasp more things and to inflict suffering on others for their own gain has reached sociopathic levels. We need to cooperate, and have empathy for one another. The war between selfishness and cooperation must be over now because we have the path to real economic freedom.

We need to work for the common good, which is good for all of us, by definition. A good example of the blindness of the self-centered focus on "me" is a huge sign over a freeway that says:

YOUR ARE NOT IN A TRAFFIC JAM
YOUR ARE THE TRAFFIC

Too many of us are hopelessly tired of our jobs, which show little hope for our own future and the future of our children and grandchildren. We need new livelihood systems that sustain us and give us more human fulfillment, physically, emotionally, and spiritually. David C. Korten, in his ground-breaking book, *The Great Turning: From Empire to Earth Community*, has laid out most of the principals for new economic arrangements and the spirit required to advance new partnerships:

"The work of the Great Turning is not to fix Empire. It is the birth of a new era that makes a choice for life, gives expression to the higher potentials of our nature, and restores to people, families and communities the power that Empire has usurped. The work is not to claim the dominator power of hierarchy for a better cause. It is to distribute power and eliminate the hierarchy."[8]

As we look for ways to give real expression to our higher values and potentials and eliminate top down hierarchy, a most positive course of action is to establish worker owned cooperatives, and especially industrial and large scale renewable energy production cooperatives. The next step, would be to form whole regions of worker/owner cooperatives working in partnership to "advance the forward days of mankind", as Buckminster Fuller [9] was fond of saying.

However, as my good friend and award winning financial advisor, Edwin Day says, "You have to show up and pay attention." Nothing worthwhile will be accomplished unless people are wise enough, strong enough and have a fire in their belly to make a better world. Of course, there will be critics who will assault these new proposals.

Arthur Schopenhauer astutely observed: "All truth passes through three stages. First, it is ridiculed. Second, it is violently opposed. Third, it is accepted as being self-evident."

PART 1

A NEW WAY OF DOING BUSINESS: WORKER OWNED SUSTAINABLE WORKPLACES— CHRISTIAN STYLE

The Shattered American Workplace Platform

American workers have had stagnated wages for over 30 years, homeownership is now difficult and defined benefit retirement pensions have been nearly eliminated or are woefully underfunded. The cash value of many 401(k) accounts for retirement have been reduced by as much as 20% to 40% due to sudden losses in the stock market. The financial sector and investors are not investing enough in American jobs in order to provide a sustainable economic system. Social Security, Medicare and Medicaid are under attack, repeatedly by dysfunctional Republican members of Congress, and therefore, the current workplace platform in America has been shattered. All across America, there is not even a dream of a just "Social Contract." Corporations have left the leadership stage in America to pursue their highest profit-making goals in "emerging markets" by pursuing the "dive to the bottom" in labor wages, across the globe.

"Creative Destruction" and Professional Job Killers

"Creative Destruction" is a term that economist, Joseph Schumpeter, is generally credited with, which describes how capitalism creates and destroys jobs by rapidly producing an improved product or process that wipes out competitors and all of their employees. Consumers buy the new product and do not buy the old one. With the acceleration of Information Technology (IT), coupled with globalization, this nasty and unnecessary process causes the destruction of millions of jobs each year. Most corporations operate on a winner-take-all basis, with no concern or requirement to make arrangements for their employees and the employees of other businesses. Obviously, this is not a moral and just way to operate an economic system because it destroys livelihoods and families on a massive scale. As we shall see, there is a viable alternative to this destructive way of doing business of the "free enterprise system".

Pope Francis wrote, "Such an economy kills." [1] The current profit-only driven business model needs to be replaced with a Mondragon-style business model.

As we shall see, the Mondragon Style Worker-Owner cooperative system operates in a different way—they transfer employees to other industries within their family of cooperatives or retrain their employees to take on new jobs created by their own research and development divisions. Worker-Owners do not like to fire themselves. Therefore, wise cooperative corporations do advanced planning and research to create and maintain livelihoods without layoffs. They operate with cooperation rather than winner-take-all competition, which has reached new levels of sociopathic job destruction around the world. What is needed is a just and caring way to provide sustainable livelihoods worldwide, and clearly, that cannot be done through the existing "free enterprise" global outsourcing for the lowest wages and the current calculated job killing economic system. We must plan ahead to eliminate "creative destruction" from the economic system, which is the current business religion of how to make higher profits.

The Mondragon Cooperative Corporation: a New Business Model

In the workplace then, we must move beyond the old separation of labor and capital, so that they can be merged in a single organization. The "we" versus "them" mentality sets up a war between egos and between "haves" and "have nots". Labor and capital must be joined together in the same enterprise so that this conflict is eliminated and transcended, as is the case in the Mondragon Worker-Owner Cooperative System. This is an example of dichotomy-transcendence, where the old ways become meaningless, as the new way rises above the old conflict, and establishes peace, justice, full communication and wholeness. Building a new America requires a fundamental change at our workplaces to achieve real economic freedom, sustainable employment and happiness. That is why it is necessary to create worker owned workplaces, with their own

3

banks and reasonable access to capital when the business requires it for expansion or survival. This old dichotomy between labor and capital has been transcended in the Mondragon Cooperative Corporation. This has been the best kept secret in economics, based on my conversations with otherwise very knowledgeable people—but no more.

The Mondragon Cooperative Corporation, based in the Basque Provinces of northern Spain, is a highly successful community-business model that is now expanding to Latin America, the United States and other countries. Mondragon, in Spain, is a worker owned and worker governed enterprise. Mondragon in Spain employs 80,000 or more people, which is about as big as Microsoft, which has 100,000 employees. Mondragon has their own manufacturing and agricultural cooperatives, supermarkets and a retail sector. Mondragon makes appliances, machine tools, auto parts, bicycles, robots and new technologies. They have a housing construction division. The Mondragon Cooperative Corporation cooperatives were organized into a group of 166 cooperatives in 1987 all working within an inter-cooperative framework that provides much of the basic necessities of life and provides a livelihood support system.

THE NUMBER OF COOPERATIVES IN EACH SECTOR (1987)

INDUSTRIAL	86
EDUCATIONAL	46
HOUSING	15
AGRICULTURAL	8
SERVICE SECTOR	4
RETAIL	1
SUPPORT	6
TOTAL	166

Source: Roy Morrison, *We Build the Road as We Travel* [2]

Mondragon Cooperative Corporation (MCC), has several research and development centers in a variety of economic sectors which create new jobs, in a dynamic manner, to introduce new technologies in a wise and sustainable development path. "Creative destruction" is not an option if we follow the Christian path of truth, love, justice, cooperation and intelligent guidance of man-made economic systems.

Clearly a new workplace platform must be developed by workers and spiritually healthy, good hearted rich people, as soon as possible, for the old workplace platform is sinking and is barely holding together. Fortunately, the framework for a new workplace platform is now becoming well-defined. It can be built side-by-side of the existing failing platform within the laws of the United States. It can be done on a large regional scale by small, medium and large businesses who are highly motivated to build a new way of life and network together. By the end of 2010, Mondragon expanded to 256 companies working in four areas: Finance, Industry, Retail and Knowledge, as detailed in Wikipedia. The Knowledge area is described by Wikipedia as follows:

"The University of Mondragon is a university of a co-operative nature, which combines the development of knowledge, skills, and values, and maintains close relations with business, especially the Co-operatives. Technological innovation is generated through the Co-operatives' own R&D departments, the Corporate Science and Technology Plan, the work of the Corporations' 12 technology centers and the Garaia Innovation Park."

"In 2009 59.4% of total turnover came from international sales. Sales resulting from the export of products abroad and production generated in 75 subsidiaries located in 17 different countries: China (13), France (9), Poland (8), Czech Republic (7), Brazil (5), Germany (4), Italy (4), United Kingdom (3), Romania (3), United States (2), Turkey (2), Slovakia (2), India (2), Thailand (1), and Morocco (1). Overall, in 2009, these 75 plants produced goods worth 3.1 billion euros and provided work for 14,506 people. The corporate industrial park in Kunshan, close to Shanghai currently houses seven subsidiaries."

Mondragon Created its own Banking System

Most importantly, Mondragon created its own banking system, *which provides internal financing.* The bank serves the worker-owners well and provides funds for the Mondragon University, job creation and the community. Mondragon's industrial cooperatives have their own research divisions and are highly advanced technologically. They have exported technology to Germany, "which is no small trick in Europe," as Professor Fred Freundlich of Mondragon University has said.

Globally, Mondragon Cooperative Corporation has 256 cooperative enterprises in more than 27 countries. Mondragon Corporation is committed to the creation of greater social wealth through customer satisfaction, job creation, technological and business development, continuous improvement, the promotion of education, care for the cooperative community and respect for the environment.

Mondragon workers have built their own businesses, banks, schools and a university. They have taken control of their communities and their lives. They have created their own worker-guided economic system. In Mondragon, they do not wave the flags of capitalism or socialism. As you will discover, they are just different. They are an on-going experiment which operates on the Christian values of truth, goodness, justice and pursuit of the common good as taught by Christ. They take care of their families and their community as they travel together down their very own experimental path. As author Roy Morrison observed in the title of his fine book on Mondragon, *We Build the Road as We Travel.*[3]

Mondragon Is Founded on Good Human Values

The Mondragon Cooperatives were originally founded by a Catholic priest, Jose Maria Arizmendiarietta and five engineers in 1956. The priest spent several years educating young people about a business model based on solidarity and participation, in harmony with Catholic social teaching, and the importance of acquiring the necessary technical knowledge to operate a cooperative enterprise. From the beginning, Mondragon was developed with a vision that is different from socialism or capitalism. Mondragon has a spiritual basis, with worker ownership, workplace democracy and policies that are designed to enhance and maintain human well-being. In Mondragon, they do not talk at all about capitalism or socialism, partly because of all of the baggage that goes with them, but mostly because Mondragon is founded on totally different values and has a different business model. Mondragon has never focused on overcoming the extremes of capitalism or socialism. It is simply considered to be a fluid experiment, of dynamic creativity centered in a community in continuous motion. Decisions are based on a balance between the needs of cooperatives for survival and expansion and the enlightened self-interest of the individual cooperators. Mondragon does not pursue a "Third Way"; it pursues its own way of economic democracy, while embracing the dignity of the human person.

The Conflict Between Capital and Labor Is Eliminated in Mondragon

It is very important to note that when workers are also owners, the continual war between those with capital and labor is eliminated. Also, boards of directors of capitalist corporations tend to pay more to investors in the company than to workers. In Mondragon, the worker/owners invest in their corporation while investing in the workers who create the wealth with appropriate pay levels.

The Ten Cooperative Principles of Mondragon Cooperatives [4]

Open Admission

The cooperative system is open to all who agree with the basic cooperative principles without regard to ethnic background, religion, political beliefs, or gender.

Democratic Organization

The Cooperative system is based upon the equality of owner-workers. The cooperative is democratically controlled on the basis of one member, one vote; its governing structures are democratically controlled and are also responsible to the general assembly or elected body.

Sovereignty of Labor

Labor is the essential transformative factor of society. The cooperatives renounce wage labor, give full power to the owner-workers to control the co-ops, give primacy to workers in distribution of surpluses, and work to extend the cooperative choice to all members of society.

Instrumental Character of Capital

Capital is basically accumulated labor and a necessary factor in business development and savings. The co-ops pay a just but limited return on capital saved or invested, a return that is not directly tied to the losses or surpluses of the co-ops. Their need for capital shall not impede the principle of open admission, but (after an initial trial period) co-op members must make a substantial, affordable, and equal financial investment in the cooperative. At present, this membership contribution is equal to a year's salary of the lowest paid member.

Self-Management

Cooperation involves both collective effort and individual responsibility. Cooperation is the development of the individual not against others but with others. Democratic control means participation in management and the on-going development of the skills needed for self-management. There must be clear information available on the co-op's operations, systematic training of owner-workers, internal promotion for management positions, and consultations and negotiations with all cooperators in organizational decisions that affect them.

Pay Solidarity

The co-ops will practice both internal and external pay solidarity. Internally, the total pay differential between the lowest-paid and the highest-paid member shall not exceed a factor of eight. In addition, compensation is comparable to that prevailing in neighboring conventional firms.

Group Cooperation

Co-ops are not isolated entities. Cooperation exists on three levels: among individual co-ops organized into groups; among co-op groups; and between the Mondragon system and other movements.

Social Transformation

Cooperation in the Mondragon system is an instrument for social transformation. As Jose Maria Arizmendiarrieta, a founder of the movement, wrote, "Cooperation is the authentic integration of people in the economic and social process that shapes a new social order; the cooperators must make this objective extend to all those who hunger and thirst for justice in the working world."

The cooperatives reinvest a ten percent portion of their surpluses in the Basque community. A significant portion goes toward new job development, to community development (through the use of social funds), to a social security system based on mutual solidarity and responsibility, and to cooperation with other institutions (such as unions).

Universal Nature

The co-ops proclaim their solidarity with all who labor for economic democracy, peace, justice, human dignity and development in Europe and elsewhere, particularly with the peoples of the Third World.

Education

Education is essential for fulfilling the basic cooperative principles. It is fundamentally important to devote sufficient human and economic resources to cooperative education, professional training, and general education of young people for the future.

At the center of Mondragon's vitality, growth and highly successful achievements is simply *sharing*. Instead of building a hierarchical system of control, they have built a big, mostly happy, sharing family, complete with family arguments. Mondragon shows how to include all stakeholders, not just the shareholders and management. Mondragon's stakeholders include worker-owners, the families, the community and the environment that provides the basis for their existence. The banking system is directed to use retirement savings and some bank profits to provide livelihoods to its members and to create jobs for future members, including their own family members.

In Mondragon, capital is subordinate to labor as a primary principle. The workers not only share the wealth of their production with each other, they share that wealth by creating jobs for others. They have grown from 50 to over 80,000 worker-owners, by sharing the wealth of their labors, primarily through maintaining the integrity of their values and principles. In other words, they have a spiritual character that embraces higher values than merely earning a livelihood and making money. They have developed a path to earn a livelihood that can be built upon to create new jobs, and communities of happiness that most of the world has not yet seen.

MCC has struggled through the ruthless "dive to the bottom for lowest wage labor" by transnational corporations so that they could obtain the lowest labor costs in the world. MCC has had to make adjustments to be able to produce and sell its products, but it has maintained its core values and principles, while growing and thriving. Greg MacLeod, in the *Harvard International Review*, describes how Mondragon actually grew when other corporations declined:

"In 2006 and 2007 most large global corporations experienced a decline in revenue. Mondragon, on the other hand, increased revenues from $15 billion to $17 billion, an increase of over 13%. In 2007, Mondragon returned over

US $50 million to workers as a share of profits. During this period, Mondragon's total workforce expanded from 83,000 to 103,000, an increase of 20,000. One reason for Mondragon's freedom of operation compared to conventional corporations is that it does not rely on stock markets for capital. Instead, it relies on its associated banks and worker shares as well as commercial loans."[4]

The main thrust of MacLeod's article is that business corporations have a duty to society to create and maintain jobs. Businesses could not function without an extensive school and university system and a huge investment in public infrastructure. The modern corporation clearly depends on government funded schools to educate their workers, provide research and development and infrastructure and therefore they have an obligation to create jobs within the United States instead of sending them abroad at slave labor wages.

In 2008, MCC reached annual sales of more than sixteen billion euros with its own cooperative university, cooperative bank, and cooperative social security mutual. It is ranked as the top Basque business group, the seventh largest in Spain, and the world's largest industrial workers cooperative.

MCC firms still must compete with traditional rivals for customers in the marketplace, and therefore, they must keep a competitive edge. MCC has two major ways to stay competitive: (1) MCC enterprises are known for high quality products through their own research divisions, and (2) they have far fewer layers of supervisors on the payroll, because they are worker-owners that exercise self-management, eliminating hated micro-management. (3) MCC does not pay obscene salaries to their top management. They pay no more than 8 times the salary of their average staff to the General Managers. These are some of the main ways MCC can sell high quality products at a competitive price. This enables MCC to be on the leading edge of the Spanish economy. However, destructive competition is a curse on all economic systems. Cooperation and sustainable livelihoods are the true path for economic systems of the future.

Income equality

As noted above, Mondragon policies only allow the salary of the CEO or General Manager to be 6 times the salary of the average worker/owner. In the case of the bank, the Caja Laboral, the salaries go up to eight times the entry level worker-owner salary because most of the top personnel in the bank have Doctorate Degrees. In the United States, CEOs are given 140 to over 350 times, or more, than what is earned by their average workers. They do not actually "earn" that much; however, they are given millions, often by themselves as managers, while the shareholders look blindly the other way. This is another factor that enables MCC to deliver a high quality product at a competitive price.

Wages, Profit Sharing and Retirement in Worker Owned Cooperatives

Mondragon businesses pay comparable salaries with other non-worker owned companies. Workers are required to invest capital in the company, generally one year's wages. Workers receive the largest share of the profits, some of which are used for company reserves, profit sharing, and about ten percent is used for charity, and Mondragon University. The average worker, who retires after 25 years, receives a $100,000 lump sum payment and a pension of 70 percent of average earnings over the last five years.

A Happier Workplace Is Possible

Mondragon does not have layer upon layer of supervisors to micro-manage the worker's work-life. Everyone is a worker-owner, and everyone is their own supervisor in general. So, when a problem comes up, workers can simply fix it. They don't blame each other. When there is a hierarchy in a business, it sets up a situation for a "blame game". Instead of focusing on *who to blame for a problem,* the worker-owners can proceed straight away *to fix it* and move on to their usual work pattern, without that hated trip to the supervisor's office. This creates a much less stressful work environment, which is good for everyone's health as well as their productivity.

The Mondragon model provides worker/owners with a good, flexible kind of workplace. For example, if a task is boring or monotonous, but required, people can work at that task for only two hours and then go on to another assignment. So, what does this do? It helps take the drudge factor out of a person's work life. One can move on to more satisfying and meaningful tasks, with the full knowledge that as a worker and owner, individuals have a real say in how the work is done.

In order to raise our "happiness index" and have a good standard of living we will need to create new worker-owned cooperatives, otherwise there is nothing to prevent corporations from making us unhappy in a "boss-subordinate" relationship that operates on fear of being fired individually, or by the tens of thousands and makes us poor in spirit and poor economically, once again.

Mondragon Is Not Socialism

A brief review of the major tenets of Socialism will show how it differs from the tenets of Mondragon: In Socialism, economic and political power is concentrated in a governing elite, a bureaucratic body of State government control. It denies economic freedom and independence of the individual. It is a non-Christian, materialistic ideology and system, which fosters the absolute dependency of all citizens on the State for their income security and well-being. Savings by individuals are used to finance ownership by the State elite and the State redistributes incomes. Prices and wages are controlled by the government. All citizens are completely under the control of the State by police power and no exceptions are allowed. No wonder this economic system of injustice and lack of caring for each other did not survive!

A word of caution: If we substitute complete control by the State with complete control by Corporations, this results in Corporate Socialism. One finds that capitalism today is very close to having complete corporate control of the election of politicians, the Supreme Court, the economy and who gets and retains a sustainable livelihood, at least for a while—as there are no guarantees of financial security in that system.

The Mondragon style of economics offers a way for investors, both internal and external, to finance the creation of sustainable livelihoods while generating enough return on investment to satisfy outside investors and to create wealth for the worker/owner's retirement. This is simply a new pathway that does not have a label; it is not state communism or socialism, nor is it state public controlled or private corporate controlled. It is more than social democracy because it has the power to advance the days of humankind in a new way, based in Christian values of truth, goodness and justice. It is time to throw away the labels of right or left, and to do what is best for the common good of humanity.

The economic framework needs to focus on the survival and advancement of the human family. As Wendell Berry said, "I must design my own economic system or be enslaved by the other man's." We have shown how to develop workable alternatives that replace what we dislike. We, as a society, need to transcend the dichotomies that divide us.

I will assert up front, with Pope Francis, that the family unit is the basic unit of all societies, both economically and spiritually. The family is the place where we can learn first to overcome our selfish egos and learn to love our spouses, children and friends in a hopefully secure and loving environment. Yes, and it is a struggle, because we have to learn to live with ourselves and other people. After all is considered, family and friends in our extended family, remain the strongest support base that enables us to grow and survive trials and hardships.

Sharing Yields Real Individual and Community Wealth

Despite the Western world's excessive individualism, there is a growing awareness of the need to cooperate and work together. Albert Nolan said, "Awareness of our oneness and solidarity leads naturally and spontaneously to a spirit of sharing. Any idea that we may be able to love one another without sharing is a romantic illusion. Once we have begun to experience ourselves as one flesh, sharing becomes as natural as feeding our own children." To illustrate the fact of our "oneness" and sharing, Nolan cites the work of geneticist Theodosius Dobzhansky and Thomas Berry who determined that "the universe in its emergence is neither determined nor random, but creative."[5]

In other words, the direction of the universe is not the step-by-step slavish implementation of a preconceived blueprint. The new scientific story of the universe supersedes Darwin's view that species evolved mainly by natural selection and mutation. Discoveries in microbiology genetics and the study of DNA reveal a far more complex process of cooperation as well as competition in the web of life. This has been well described in ecosystems, which are systems within systems, all working together to provide a food chain among plants and animals, resulting in survival in a supportive complex of interactions.

Many scientists now see the unfolding of the universe as a continual creative process, beginning with the Big Bang. "Everything, but everything, has evolved out of that singularity: matter and spirit, atoms and stars, chemicals and life forms, you and me. It was Teilhard de Chardin, who first pointed out that the spirit or consciousness must have been present from the beginning because there is no matter without spirit of some kind. Discoveries in biology have led to the conclusion that DNA is essentially a code of information. Information can only come from a person's consciousness and information can be more than facts, as it can contain meaning and purpose. For example, the statement "The British are coming," is only four bits of information, but the meaning content was huge for Americans. The philosophy of science has reached the understanding that our DNA coded information came from an Intelligent Designer, with an astonishing creative capacity. Stephen C. Meyer's book, *Signature in the Cell: DNA and the Evidence for Intelligent Design*, is a major scientific breakthrough.[6]

In his insightful work, *Living Systems*,[7] James G. Miller shows that all living systems have a sub-system he described as a decider or selector sub-system. Even an amoeba decides whether it will move forward or backward. This may be called "instinct", at the amoeba level, and that may be true. But the rudimentary function is some form of "mental activity". At some point in the continuing creative process of the development of consciousness, humankind took a great leap forward. Beatrice Bruteau describes human consciousness this way:

"We experience our consciousness *subjectively*, as subjects, from the inside. All other levels of organization we observed from the outside, objectively seeing them as objects of our cognition. But in the case of our own consciousness, we do something more than, and quite different from knowing it as an object for our cognition. We know it by being it."[8]

You won't find consciousness in the brain, because consciousness has qualities that cannot be explained by neurons and synapses in the billions or brain scans of those physical structures.

Albert Nolan wrote: "Our consciousness, and therefore our subjectivity, cannot be explained, because it is a primary datum. It cannot be explained by reference to anything more simple or primary. The mystery deepens at every turn. The mystery of our evolving universe is a mystery of mind-boggling unity or oneness. As humans we are one flesh belonging to one human family."[9]

What the scientific study of evolution enables us to appreciate, all the better, is that the Creator is not like a human manufacturer of goods. God is more like an artist. The universe is not the implementation of a predetermined blueprint, but the magnificent ongoing result of artistic creativity. For that reason too, each of us is unique—a unique work of art. This is how God loves us, by giving us the human dignity of a unique person. It has been estimated that 108 billion people have been born on the Planet Earth. The fact that we, as human beings, are all unique is proof that the Creator gave us our individuality out of love for our being as a beloved person. We are all evolving in a continuous creative process, which of course, necessarily calls for a Creator. Most importantly, we are co-creators with God. As Abraham Maslow, the wise psychologist pointed out, we now know that we are responsible for our own evolution. We have to do our part.

Albert Nolan wrote: "The scientific evidence provides us with an opportunity to experience something of God's mysterious and continuous creativity in all its variety and beauty. We see the glory of God in the grandeur of a creatively evolving universe."[10]

As we grow in our experience of togetherness and inseparability, we begin to direct all we do and say toward what we call the *common good.* What that means in practice is that we come to see that what is best for everyone is best for us too. There is no possible conflict between our good and the common good. Sharing follows quite naturally from this. There would be no reason to force people to share.

Why Socialism Failed

Albert Nolan describes why socialism failed: "The fundamental mistake of the socialist countries of the last century was that they forced whole nations to share when the overwhelming majority of the people did not want to share (under total State control). That is counterproductive and oppressive."[11] To enter into a broader kind of sharing in the Mondragon worker-owner cooperatives, one enters on a temporary basis for one year, studies it, and decides if that common good is what they want. New jobs are offered with the clear understanding that they must be sustainable jobs in the foreseeable future. However, once a worker-owner, the worker can transfer to other jobs that have emerged in the cooperatives over time. Of course, worker-owners can stay or leave of their own free will. Mondragon endeavors to operate at a higher calling level, a spiritual community level that involves sharing, transcending one's selfish ego and learning to experience "oneness" with a human family of worker-owners, while balancing the individual growth and income needs with the good of each individual and the whole community.

Mondragon Has Come to America

The Mondragon Cooperative Corporation has established the framework in which the Good Person can work in the Good Society in Spain, Europe, Asia, South America and now, at last, the United States. Mondragon has entered into a collaborative agreement with the United Steel Workers. The United Auto Workers have also agreed to develop Mondragon style worker/ owner cooperatives. As we shall see, the foundations for launching thousands of new industrial and service cooperatives is already here, in the United States. It will take time and its forward progress rests mostly with this current generation, which has embraced networking and economic justice, as demonstrated in the Occupy Wall Street movement and social interaction on the Internet.

However, in the United States, the development of the Good Society needs a regional and local model in order to demonstrate how Americans can make the secure shift from the current failed and dying workplace platform to a new life-giving workplace platform and a healthy community. The Mondragon model needs to be advanced in the U.S., and adapted to meet American cultural needs. The Mondragon model can be expanded with new livelihood systems that are home grown.

Towards a Regional System of Sustainable Job Creation

Worker/owner businesses can be established on a local and regional basis, which can be grouped together to provide economic opportunities and far more financial security. In order to provide and maintain enough employment for all, it will be necessary to do long range planning on a regional level. Each region has different ways to produce renewable energy. Energy replaces the hard physical labor by driving machines and it drives machines that make machines. The engineers in Mondragon manufacture appliances and machines that drive machines. They design and build robots and supply technology for automotive production. Mondragon has shown us how we can grow in the art of sustainable job creation rather than job destruction.

However, the ideal of long range planning on a regional level in different parts of a country such as the U.S. will require a new educational path of regional planning for each unique region. Long Range Regional Plans can be developed to achieve sustainable nation building at home across the US. One way to begin this process is to create programs at the Master Degree level for each region of the country, starting with the basic ways that renewable energy can be produced, be it wind, solar thermal, photovoltaic panels, geothermal, hydro and hydrogen storage which can be transformed back into electricity. In Part 5, we will examine the advantages of

25

Satellite New Town development within a 30-45 minute rapid transit ride to the employment centers in major cities. As we shall see, Satellite New Town planning on a regional scale can provide very positive solutions to a whole range of interlocking problems. These New Towns can be the centers of energy development for that particular region as well as a way to create sustainable employment for the coming generation and immigrants.

In the 1950's, before the outsourcing of our manufacturing base, most Americans had jobs that counted for something of value—they grew food, made and sold products that people needed to survive or to improve their lives, or performed critical services. That was a meaningful economy and all the people involved in it could feel good about their jobs. With Long Range Regional Planning we can create that kind of sustainable, secure and happy economic system. We do that, in part, by manufacturing things that people need and want to survive and flourish.

"Today, most people work jobs that are far removed from the necessities of life. They make frivolous gizmos, or they "manage money", or they shuffle papers, or they sell people stuff they don't need. The work provides no intrinsic rewards, so people try to fill the hole by buying as much stuff as they can with the paychecks those jobs earn. This isn't a "feminine" economy. It's a meaningless one and every man and woman trapped in it feels useless and empty." (This is a quote from a column in *The Palm Beach Post,* written by a columnist whose column was anonymous called "The Practical Man". One way out of this trap is to build regional economies that provide the basic necessities of life in worker-owner cooperatives through long range planning.

The Mondragon model will be explored in more detail, and especially its key guidance system: a worker-owned banking system, which takes money and turns it into Labor-Wealth, distributed back to those who produce the wealth as a just society would happily do. This is a new economic arrangement simply beyond the realms of Socialism or Capitalism. The current financial system of banks and Wall Street no longer meet worker's needs of local investment in sustainable economics and development, or sustainable livelihoods. The Mondragon Banking System provides strong answers to these issues.

The Mondragon Style Banking System

One of the biggest advantages to businesses, who sign on to the Mondragon Style Cooperative way of doing business, is that they can have access to capital when it is needed to expand, re-train, or survive. As every businessman knows, making payroll is sometimes very difficult. Mondragon broke the selfish rules of the times when they established their very own sustainable community building banking system.

The Mondragon bank, Caja Laboral, offers a model of strength for existing cooperatives and refined management for start-up businesses as well. The Banking Division undertakes the community building and integrative work of the cooperatives. The Banking Division accumulates financial resources, which the cooperators understand as accumulated labor wealth, not accumulated capital wealth. This accumulated worker-wealth is partially used for sharing profits and to create more jobs, including jobs for the sons and daughters of the cooperators. In this way, the bank is truly a community bank and is at the very heart of Mondragon's success, because it advances the forward days of the families and the entire community in which the cooperators live.

The Empresarial Division utilizes the accumulated worker-wealth to undertake the sustainable job-creation expansion and the embracing of economic freedom that is the dynamic life energy of the whole enterprise. The bank assists in making a business plan and then carefully tracks the needs of that business, supplying the knowledge, expertise and resources to become a healthy and stable enterprise. "The Caja Laboral has helped Mondragon cooperatives succeed in the particularly difficult task of actualizing the often hollow freedoms promised by economic and political liberalism. The elaboration of the cooperative system leads to the convergence between the practice of democracy and the building of community. Freedom in this context includes the right to make agreements, but becomes much more than a narrow economic or political abstraction, or the largely theoretical (and often violated) rights of isolated and powerless individuals."[12]

The Mondragon experience provides a refreshing contrast to the enormous disparity between so-called "freedom", under the current so-called "free market system", and the reality of working life. In Mondragon, contracts and agreements are made by all affected, with one man having one vote. The individual actually votes for far more freedom in his or her working arrangements, while balancing the worker's needs with productivity and the need of the cooperators community to grow, thrive and survive. In Mondragon, this is called "the search for equilibrio."[13] Striving for "equilibrio" is truly where extreme egos must learn to become mature, caring human beings. Most of all it means sharing with your fellow worker-owners and also with the larger community outside of the Mondragon family. It is not an easy balancing act, but it is at the heart of what makes Mondragon a vibrant, thriving and caring enterprise.

Cooperatives Invest Retirement Savings Back Into Cooperatives Not Wall Street

In January 2009, there were $2.5 trillion in 401(k) retirement savings plans, according to the non-profit Employee Benefit Research Institute. Imagine the investment power that those funds would give Mondragon Style cooperatives. Instead of risking money in stocks and bonds and Wall Street bubbles, cooperators would be investing in their own growth, while securing their own, more secure retirement in old age.

Between October 2007 and October 2008, there were 50 million 401(k) account holders who suffered major losses as $1.0 trillion was lost in stock values, as estimated by the Employee Benefit Research Institute. This has been a really heart-breaking loss to all, and especially, to people who were close to retirement.

As long as corporations, Wall Street, and the international banking cartel have access to the retirement funds of workers, Americans do not have financial security even for retirement. However, if workers invest retirement funds in worker-owned Mondragon Style cooperative banks they can be assured of far more financial security. Workers can take charge of their workplace life, their investments, their community and retirement.

There is a detailed account of Mondragon's annual growth from 1979 to 1986 of 11%, as compared to the average 6% annual growth in the United States, contained in Roy Morrison's excellent book on Mondragon, *We Build the Road as We Travel.*[14]

It is the special way that the Mondragon bank guides the whole system that keeps the cooperators on the right path of "seeking the good of all", themselves included. *The first and most important step in creating new cooperatives on a community or regional scale is to establish a Mondragon Style banking system.*

How to Establish a Mondragon Style Banking System in America

Small and medium-sized businesses comprise about 50% of the economic system and they produce approximately 80% of all new jobs, according to the Department of Labor. With the establishment of a Mondragon Style banking system, funded by cooperative members, many small and medium sized business owners who need capital and guidance to expand will find that signing a contract to join a Constellation of businesses, with a worker-owner charter and a nourishing banking system can be highly inviting.

Germany Has 1,116 Co-operative Banks

Germany has 1,116 co-operative banks that are flourishing, according to *The Economist magazine.* These co-operative banks have come through the financial crisis with barely a scratch so far. "They argue that their business model, working for the public or mutual good rather than for shareholders, is well suited to the mixture of households and small companies (known as *Mittelstand*) that they serve. The savings banks and co-operative banks provide about two-thirds of all lending to *Mittelstand* companies and 43% of lending to all companies and households."[15]

In the U.S. there is already an "umbrella" national banking system for cooperatives. The National Cooperative Bank (NCB), is known for providing creative financial solutions tailored to meet the needs of cooperatives, nationwide. The NBC Financial Group (NCB) consists of the National Consumer Cooperative Bank, a federally chartered cooperative corporation; its wholly-owned subsidiary NCB, FSB, a federally chartered savings bank; and, NCB Capital Impact, a 501(c)(3) non-profit affiliate. Loans and other financial services are provided by NCB, FSB, and NCB Capital Impact. Deposit products and services are provided by NCB, FSB, which is a member of the Federal Deposit Insurance Corporation (FDIC). Each is a separate corporation within the NCB Financial Group. The NCB Annual Report describes the cooperatives that it works with as follows:

"Although similar to other business models, a cooperative has several unique features. It is owned and controlled by its members who have joined together to use the cooperative's goods, services and facilities. A board of directors, elected by the membership, sets the cooperative's policies and procedures. By pooling resources, members can leverage their shared power to buy, sell, market, or bargain as one group, achieving economies of scale and sharing in any profits generated. In addition, communities benefit both socially and fiscally by the cooperatives' ability to access and deliver goods and services across the nation."

The NCB operates like other banks, except that it is dedicated to strengthening communities, with a special focus on cooperative expansion and economic development. Having said that, while the NCB may provide a national umbrella of financial services, nation-wide, it does not operate the same way as the Caja Laboral, which as we have seen, is the heart of the Mondragon cooperatives' community building enterprise.

The Caja Laboral is much more regionally focused and is strongly involved in community building and new job creation within their region in Spain. As noted, it has an Empresarial Division, which focuses on launching and assisting new start-ups. In a Regional development model, those start-ups would be most favored which aim to make the region self-sufficient in the basic necessities of life, i.e., energy, food, water, construction/ shelter, transportation, healthcare, hardware and forestry, lumber, research and cooperative education in human values. The production of solar energy and wind power are essential for most regions. Energy is also the most needed commodity nationally as the energy crunch deepens when oil prices rise. Having met the basic necessities, a region can always focus on exporting energy in order to purchase luxury goods that it cannot yet produce or does not want to produce. The demand for clean renewable energy will always be high as we move through the 21st century.

Commerce, Creativity, Inventions and Dynamic Job Security Management

The economist Joseph Schumpeter described the process of creativity and inventions in the business world as "creative destruction", because new inventions by one firm can be such an improvement above the product of another firm that the latter is put out of business. But it doesn't have to be that way. Mondragon has its own research and development organization to advance new inventions within the family of cooperatives, thereby maintaining jobs while staying on the leading edge of industrial processes and leading technology. Over time, economic systems need to evolve to a more creative and sustaining workplace platform that give people more personal financial security. Mondragon style economics is dynamic *and* sustaining.

The Empresarial Division of MC works with the newly forming cooperative to create a well-developed and sophisticated business plan, which can take up to two years. Then, the cooperative business is tracked to ensure that it is growing and has all that it needs to thrive and survive. This is a dynamic, sustaining process that gives new life to the local community and the region as a whole. Most business start-ups in the competitive free market system die out within five years. The two major reasons for failure are: (1) lack of capital when it is needed in a timely manner and (2) poor management decisions. The Caja Laboral tracks the new cooperative and when it sees signs of danger, it moves in to assist and sustain. It may be occasionally necessary to shift an entire industrial team to a new product line. In this manner, cooperator's jobs are maintained rather than destroyed and eliminated. This is a major, necessary improvement over the "dog-eat-dog" style of capitalism that is so destructive to human well-being today.

The Caja Laboral, in conjunction with the worker-owners' Governing Council, also has the extremely important role of maintaining balance between the needs and desires of individuals and the community as a whole, also known as "equilibrio". This is a very special kind of a hands-on bank. It is given the profits of the cooperators to manage and distribute according to the expressed will of the members; it invests some of these funds and earns interest, historically with an 8% average return on investment. The bank creates local jobs and helps sustain them and nurtures their growth, largely using the retirement savings of Mondragon employees. However, as long as Mondragon must be assaulted by capitalistic corporations, it will suffer through some trials.

How to Get Out of the Stock Market: Invest In Energy Producing Cooperatives

Americans are told by virtually all financial counselors to continue to invest in the stock market. They all advise American workers to diversify across multiple investment lines, consider your risk tolerance and invest regularly to take advantage of dips and rises in stock prices. They have advised Americans to stay in the stock market even through the Reagan Era Bust, the Dot-com Bust, and the colossal Housing Fraud Bust. Financial advisors told us to stay in the market *all of the way down to a loss of as much as 40% of our paper savings in the stock market!* Those who have 401(K) accounts can simply move their investments into cash, with no taxation or penalty. Many employees are unaware of this fact because many financial advisors do not advise employees to get out of the market and protect what they have saved.

Today, with money market funds at 2% or lower, and real estate being risky, Americans see themselves between a rock and a hard place. However, when you work in an advanced Mondragon style cooperative, the cooperators bank can maintain a 7% to 11% return on your retirement savings. This is especially true for energy producing cooperatives, because energy will always be in demand. In this manner, a worker-owner can be far more certain of a comfortable retirement. The driving forces of unaffordable oil costs and climate change from too much CO_2 will drive us quickly to alternative green energy development, or we simply perish. So, when cooperatives focus on solar, wind and green energy, with hydrogen storage, and hydrogen powered cars as their primary export products, they will find a strong and reliable demand for their production.

As Mondragon Style cooperatives grow in the U.S. and larger scale regional cooperatives are formed similar to those in Mondragon, Spain, the cooperatives may well decide to adopt this hands-on banking system. It will be up to the cooperators and the NCB to decide if their financial group wants to have regional banks that operate following the excellent model presented by the Caja Laboral.

General Motor's Union Should Transform the Company to Become a Mondragon-Style Cooperative

The largest American automobile manufacturer, General Motors (GM), went bankrupt in 2009 and the Obama Administration wisely made it partly nationalized in order to save the jobs of the company and its suppliers. This action was critical to avoid massive layoffs during a deep recession. GM has come back with a gain of 2.5 million dollars in 2011. The GM union bought a substantial amount of its stock, so it is clear that the union has a strong say in GM's future. According to an article provided by www.aciamericas.coop, some workers in the General Motors union wanted to turn the company into a cooperative following the Mondragon experience. It is clear that workers see the value of the Mondragon-style cooperative as a hopeful path in the future. This is not a dream any longer. It is a new awakening to our nation's future path.

Top Producing Cooperatives Had Revenues of $175.6 Billion in the U.S.

In its Annual Report, NCB posted that the top 100 revenue producing cooperative businesses had revenues of $175.6 billion in 2009. The entire NCB Co-op 100 report is available under the publications section at www.ncb.coop.

The NCB Annual report also described the power and reach that cooperatives have already established:

"In addition to generating $500 billion in revenue, cooperatives directly employ 500,000 people across the country, and including indirect and induced effects, support more than two million jobs nationwide. As many sectors absorb the slowing activity of the current economic conditions, cooperatives and its members often fare better in challenging times than investor-owned firms, due to its adaptable structure and governing body. Cooperatives can more readily adjust to market conditions. As a result, cooperatives are organized to maximize returns and are prepared to weather a down turn, like today's current marketplace."

"Cooperative entities exist in a cross section of sectors, including agriculture, grocery, hardware and lumber, finance, energy and communications, housing, recreation and others. Many of the cooperatives on the NCB Co-op 100 list are household names such as Land O' Lakes, Inc., Ocean Spray and Ace Hardware Corporation and Publix Super Markets with

1,000 stores. Today, there are more than 30,000 cooperatives in the United States that account for more than 73,000 places of business."

Mondragon Has Come to America: United Steel Workers Collaborate with the World's Most Advanced Worker-Owned Cooperative

On October 27, 2009, The United Steelworkers (USW) and Mondragon International, S.A., signed a framework agreement for collaboration in establishing Mondragon cooperatives in the manufacturing sector within the United States and Canada. The USW and Mondragon will work to establish manufacturing cooperatives that will adopt the worker ownership model of one worker, one vote.

USW International President, Leo W. Gerard, said: "We see today's agreement as a historic first step towards making union co-ops a viable business model that can create good jobs, empower workers, and support communities in the United States and Canada. Too often we have seen Wall Street hollow out companies by draining their cash and assets and hollowing out communities by shedding jobs and shuttering plants. We need a new business model that invests in workers and invests in communities."

Employee Stock Ownership Plans Are Not Worker Owner Cooperatives

Highlighting the differences between Employee Stock Ownership Plans (ESOPS) and union co-ops, Gerard said, "We have lots of experiences with ESOPs, but have found that it doesn't take long for the Wall Street types to push workers aside and take back control. We see Mondragon's cooperative model with 'one worker', 'one vote' ownership as a means to re-empower workers and make business accountable to Main Street instead of Wall Street."

Josu Ugarte, President of Mondragon International said, "What we are announcing today represents a historic first— combining the world's largest industrial worker cooperative with one of the world's most progressive and forward-thinking manufacturing unions to work together so that our combined know-how and complimentary visions transform manufacturing practices in North America."

Ugarte also said, "…the Steelworkers who have proved time and time again that the future belongs to those who connect vision and values to people and put all three first."

How to Start a Cooperative Enterprise in Your Region Ownership Associates, Inc.

Ownership Associates, Inc., based in Cambridge Massachusetts, is a consulting company serving the needs of employee ownership companies. They can advise on how to start a new cooperative enterprise or how to make an existing business into a new cooperative. For details, see their website. Email: oa@ownershipassociates.com

Fred Freundlich, is a principal with Ownership Associates, Inc. and he is a professor in Mondragon University in the faculty of Business Science. Fred Freundlich is an American, who lives in Spain and he is a doctoral candidate at Harvard University, at this writing. He has made presentations on Mondragon which are highly recommended videos, available on the Internet. Professor Freundlich, as a principal with Ownership Associates, can offer ways to link more directly with the Mondragon bank and technology organizations within Mondragon.

The United Steel Workers (USW)

The USW is proceeding cautiously with cooperative start-ups, at this writing, according to Rob Witherell at his Organizing Department's offices in the USW headquarters in Pittsburgh. "We've made a commitment here, but for that reason, we want to make sure we get it right, even if it means starting slowly and on a modest scale."

USW is looking for viable small businesses in appropriate sectors where the current owners are interested in selling and cashing out. The union is also looking for financial institutions with a focus on productive investment, such as cooperative banks and credit unions. "It can get complicated," Witherell said, "Not only do you have to fund the buyout, but you also have to figure out how to lend workers the money to buy-in, so they can repay it at a reasonable rate over a period of time, and still make a decent living." However, if we establish regional Mondragon style banks, we can move aggressively to establish regional worker-owner cooperatives.

The National Cooperative Bank (NCB Financial Group)

The NCB is well described above. Location of banks can be found on the NCB website under the NCB Story.

Providential Providers: A Source of Capital for Cooperatives

The Mondragon success story has a major achievement to share with the world at large: it shows what wise, good-hearted investors can do. There is a world of difference between a capitalist who is solely seeking bigger profits and a "wise capitalizer" who has the best interests of people and families at heart and can still make a good, reliable return of 8% or more on his or her investment.

Capitalizers with wisdom are needed for a wholly new banking system. Investors are needed as new town builders, along with government financial support, primarily to build a new renewable energy system and infrastructure. I call them "providential providers", who will be using their money for good purposes and they will have their just and due financial rewards, as well as abundant spiritual rewards. How will that be arranged, you may ask, and the answer is by pro-active invitation to millionaires and billionaires, investors and bankers to participate in an enterprise that gives them an 8% return on investment and much, much more in spiritual returns.

One may then ask "How will all of this be accomplished in financial and technical terms? The answer is to establish Mondragon Style Banks across the nation, so that worker-owners can invest their own money, including trillions of retirement savings, to create more jobs in more cooperatives. Private investors, credit unions and the nation's good will banks need to be invited to lead and assist in this massive national re-construction and retro-fitting plan.

Banking Needs to Advance the Livelihoods and Well-Being of Humankind

In 2010, the Bank of International Settlements reported that there were 614 trillion dollars in Derivatives and Credit Default Swaps. The whole production of goods and services per year in the U.S. only amounts to $14 to $15 trillion. It is not clear what the share of this 614 trillion is purchased by the U.S. corporations, but it is clear that the whole world market economy is insuring against potential, undefined losses in a treacherous "free market system".

This kind of insurance, if necessary, should be bought simply as insurance, according to George Soros, a leading hedge fund manager, who testified before a Congressional

Committee. In order to provide real capital for rebuilding America at home, the United States government needs to levy a tax on derivatives and credit swaps, as the European Union is considering at this writing. A very small tax of one percent on these financial transactions can provide 6 trillion dollars for deficit reduction and nation building at home. We may also wonder why these casinos should be allowed to exist at all as they take money out of the pool for investment in job creation. Europe is now considering to totally separate standard loans for local investment from banking that invests in the "casino" of derivatives and credit default swaps. In the U.S. that would be equivalent to the reinstatement of the Glass-Steagall act that protected Americans from the financial disaster that occurred in 2008 and has not yet been totally corrected.

Reducing the Risk of the "Free Market Economy"

However, even better, let us all reduce the threat of incredible losses in the potentially devastating "free market economy." This is clearly a gambling casino, based on the premise of fear. Fear of major losses and failure in the "free market" economic structure has now reached mammoth proportions of over 614 trillion dollars in derivatives and credit default swaps. We can safely conclude that it is way past time to take these incredible risks, uncertainties and ghosts of fear out of the "free market competitive economy" by establishing a cooperative, sharing and sustainable economy.

Clearly, the "free market economic structure" has failed to provide security to large public pension funds and corporate pension funds, and to the families of the world, which are the rock foundation of all societies. That is why it is urgent to implement a new economic structure that works for all of us. Mondragon Style Cooperatives and the development of other new economic arrangements offers a new path to reduce fear from the nation's economic system and to provide a far more secure future for families as the basic unit of a caring civilized world.

Instead of bankers making money by trading in their gambling casino, some, who are enlightened and are good people can become "providential providers", and invest in Mondragon Style Cooperatives which produce energy and advance the forward days of humankind and still make money at a good return on investment.

Many good hearted billionaires, such as Bill and Linda Gates, Warren Buffet, George Soros, Roger Lewis, Ted Turner and many others, have already given billions to help improve the lot of humankind, often in the health sector. Mondragon-style corporations offers a whole new path for billionaires with vision to be providential providers in building Satellite New Towns to develop solar and wind energy with a new and happier way of life for millions of people, while saving the nation from the ravages of Climate Change. Again, what we have been seeking is in our midst. It is here and now, alive in this world, as the ships of Capitalism and Socialism sink into a sea of total dysfunction, because they have not been willing to share of their own free will.

The rich and powerful now have a golden opportunity to advance the forward days of humankind. The rich have enticed lawmakers to build a vast network of tax laws and banking practices, by financing their campaigns and their very livelihood. This elaborate structure is designed to enable them to amass piles of money and to keep it to themselves. It is time to seek wisdom and learn how to love humanity.

One person observed that the largest banker's business plan is *grand theft.* It is the frightened building of a structure to give the rich a sense of security, when in fact, there is little security in this life unless one has good values and character against what Shakespeare called "the slings and arrows of outrageous misfortune". In my understanding of reality, it is God's demonstrated love for us, in which, alone, our real security rests.

Throughout history, the building of an Empire is the insecure act of the rich to keep their riches and then the building of military power to keep other Empires from invading and taking their treasures. This is the way the world looked when Jesus took center stage in the face of the mighty Roman Empire and Albert Nolan described the situation well:

"He did not simply want to replace those in power with others who were not yet in power. He was looking at something more radical than that. He took the values of his time, in all their variety, and turned them on their heads. He was busy with a *social* revolution, rather than a *political* one, a social revolution that called for a deep spiritual conversion.

"A social revolution is one that turns the social relations between people in a society upside down. A political revolution is one that changes the power relations in a society by overthrowing one government and replacing it with another. Jesus, like most other oppressed Jews in his time, saw that everyone wanted political liberation from Roman oppression. But he saw himself as a prophet whose immediate mission was the introduction of a social and spiritual revolution. The dismantling of the structures of power would follow later."[16] The social and spiritual revolution that Jesus taught is, of course, still underway. However, globally, we have made some progress. People around the world generally think that the people of other nations are just like themselves: basically good, willing to share some of their wealth, if they have any, with those who have little or nothing. Face to face, human beings are very much alike. Their lives are mostly centered on their families and their work. They want peace, justice and a stable livelihood. They have compassion for those who are in distress because of fire caused by droughts, and historically unheard of floods, tornados and hurricanes, which are increasing in intensity because of climate change, also described by someone as "global weirding".

It is the ego-driven policies of certain nations that the people do not like, as demonstrated by the shows on Link TV (Television Without Borders), who produced "The Listening Project", where journalists traveled around the world and asked people open questions, such as: "What do you think of America?" A shocking question for a journalist to ask on camera, for all to see!

They discovered that it was not the *people of America* they dislike; it was the military and economic policies of American politicians that they don't like, and the leaders who create and perpetuate those destructive-to-life policies. This TV show is available on The Dish and by viewing Link TV shows on the Internet. These shows from around the world clearly demonstrate that the human family is ONE. We are nearly all alike at the human family level, once the false self of the ego is taken into account and the implementers of evil policies and practices are understood, protested against and replaced as the revolutions around the globe are demonstrating. The Mondragon Style of working and living offers a way to achieve a social and spiritual revolt. I use the term "revolt" because a revolt is *a successful revolution* and Mondragon has succeeded with a social and economic revolt without loss of life, or even much political confrontation. The Mondragon enterprise is appreciated in Spain. However, with the latest revolution in the streets of Spain, we see that the Mondragon Style of economics has not been realized and embraced by all Spanish economists, investors and political leaders. Also, Spain has a 25% unemployment rate, largely due to the global financial crisis and the housing bubble burst.

While many nations have leaders who have not learned Jesus' teachings "to love your enemies"; "to turn the other cheek" and not take revenge; and forgiving them all "seventy times seven times", people who see themselves as part of the human family can begin to embrace such hard sayings, because they can see the power of love. We can see that caring for each other is best, especially in a world that is growing in distress. Christ's last teaching, "As I have loved you, love one another" tells us clearly what to do. Christ points out that Christ and the Father love us first.

Even a more radical teaching in Jewish times was what Jesus said about the rich and the poor, which brings home *the need to share*, as they have learned to do in Mondragon. In the Sermon on the Mount, Jesus said, "Blessed are you who are poor," (Luke 6:20). Then, he said, "Woe to you that are rich" (Luke 6:24).

The prevailing assumption, at the time, was that God had blessed the rich with wealth, which made them the most fortunate. Jesus stood tall and said that just the opposite is true. Again, Albert Nolan clarifies this radical teaching best: "In other words, it is not the rich who are blessed and fortunate, but the poor. This does not mean that it is good to be destitute and in need. Nor is it a promise that one day the poor will be rich. It means you should regard yourselves as fortunate that you are not among the rich and the wealthy. It is those who are rich that are the unfortunate ones. It is they who should be pitied because it is they who are going to find it very difficult to live in the world of the future (the Kingdom of God) where everything will be shared. The rich will find it very difficult to share in this world and the next. They will be like camels trying to get through the eye of a needle. The poor are the fortunate because they will find it easy to share."[17]

Why is this teaching so very real and critical today? It is so hard for the very wealthy to share their wealth, so we can hardly count on most of them to go through a deep spiritual conversion, however, some will open their hearts to God. Many of them are enslaved by their wealth. The extremely rich wake up in the morning and they must decide (1) how to protect their massive wealth, properties and things from being stolen; (2) how to invest their wealth so that they gain millions more and do not lose millions in the process; (3) what to buy next, in terms of pleasing the spouse, collecting new treasures on Earth, and when to throw a lavish party to engage with other rich people; (4) perhaps, maintain the sea going yacht; (5) to count and re-count their piles of money, gold bullion, stocks and bonds; (6) determine how much to donate to charities. There is never a chance for a thought about giving away 50% to 90% of their wealth and living very, very well on the remaining amount. Most of the rich are truly enslaved by their money and worldly cares to even consider the true values of life, namely, caring about others who are in need.

However a few billionaires, such as Bill and Linda Gates, Warren Buffet and Ted Turner have given billions to aid the poor, which has been a good-hearted endeavor. Their free act of will was to share some of their wealth with those who desperately needed what they could provide.

The acts of sharing, then, may be mainly in the hands of the middle class and the poor. The social revolution must largely come from the bottom up, just as it has in the Mondragon cooperatives and most recently from protests in the Middle East, Europe and the Occupy Wall Street movement. Again, what we have been waiting for is in our midst. The model is well defined and highly successful, but it has self-confessed flaws.

Mondragon Is Not a Utopia

Roy Morrison writes, "Mondragon is not a high-minded utopian projection of the world as it should be—quite the contrary. The Caja Laboral Popular, like the rest of the Mondragon system, arose from a very sober reflection upon the world as it was and could be by Arizmendiarreta and the Mondragon cooperators."[18]

Mondragon style cooperatives are not for everyone. People who have obtained a college education, and have risen in the capitalist system, may have achieved a high level of expertise and they may want to be rewarded for their work with more money and prestige than other workers. Those people might want to stay in the capitalist system, even though they are threatened with fear of making a mistake or being fired because of "creative destruction" by a competitor.

In Mondragon, such workers would be rewarded for their contribution to the whole organization, with profit-sharing and recognition but not with the big individual monetary rewards. In that sense, Mondragon is more like a spiritual calling, where people join to have sustainability, where work is done to benefit all and to have a good, strong community life that is fulfilling in more spiritual family and community ways.

Work is still work in the cooperatives, and there is a certain peer pressure to pull your own weight as a worker-owner. Those who do not want to work as much as others, or have extreme, overly self-centered egos will simply leave the system. Economic democracy is a messy, messy business, as one can imagine. Certainly, there are arguments, and plenty of them. Fred Freundlich, an American and a professor at Mondragon University, and Mikel Lezamiz, the Director of Education, told the story of Mondragon at conferences in several American cities, and they let us know, "We are not in Heaven. We are not angels. Our people are argumentative." (See the videos of their presentation by finding Mondragon videos on the Internet. Also, see an excellent presentation on Praxis Peace.com by their president, Georgia Kelly, after she and a team visited Mondragon in Spain.)

The cooperatives provide job security, retraining, comparable wages, a democratic, caring workplace, a caring community, and a comfortable retirement. The Mondragon style cooperatives lead the world in providing a good workplace and in providing a good community. But it is not a Utopia, partly because sacrifices must be made from time to time during hard economic times. After all, Mondragon must still operate within the cruel, bottom line profiteers of globalization. Wages and hours have been cut by 5% to 10% for a limited period of time, but by mutual agreement, not by an administrative dictatorship. This is done to spread the misery on a more equitable basis, yet retain their jobs and provide the means to move forward in a challenging global economic situation.

Mondragon hires employees to meet its labor requirements with the full understanding that those who are newly hired are not eligible for membership unless their jobs can be secured as being economically viable, according to an analysis by Bernard Marszalek. Marszalek writes for a grassroots economics group in the San Francisco Bay Area, called "Just, Alternative, Sustainable Economics," and he attended a conference on Mondragon in Sonoma, California. While participation is open to all for jobs in Mondragon some workers may not be able to become worker-owners, because new jobs must be created that are economically viable in the foreseeable future. Yet, once you are a member, after a year as a temporary worker, your job is secured. If need be, you can be transferred to another cooperative where your work is totally viable economically, or receive skill set training as required to join another cooperative.

Marszalek admires the Mondragon Cooperative, and is a strong advocate, however, he described strategic actions by Mondragon that show how difficult it is to sustain its cooperative principles while being in competition with capitalistic businesses. Competition is not such a problem in the Basque regional operation, however, when Mondragon expanded internationally into Europe, Latin America and Asia, to compete with other globalizing businesses, certain bottom line business decisions were required.

Marszalek cites the following case of dealing with capitalistic corporations:

"In the early 90's Mondragon learned that a large French retailer planned to open Wal-Mart size "big box" stores in Spain. Since Mondragon has a large domestic appliance presence in Spain, to lose retail outlets to a foreign operator threatened their national distribution. To prevent these foreign acquisitions, Mondragon began buying up various retail chains throughout Spain. For Mondragon to expand beyond its manufacturing base was a major corporate decision. And it was also significant for MCC to absorb thousands of employees throughout Spain in traditional capitalist enterprises. About ten years ago co-op membership was opened up to these new retail workers on a limited basis to ease the transition into the corporation, but the job growth of these retail outlets was outstripping the rate at which membership was attained. So early this year Mondragon decided to open up membership to all of the 40,000 retail employees. This appears to be a successful policy." Mondragon is going through a major adjustment period because of Chinese competition, with low slave labor costs, which has cut into Mondragon's home appliance market.

A Political Revolution Is Not Needed to Build Cooperative Enterprises

Roy Morrison, in his outstanding book about Mondragon, *We Build the Road as We Travel*, stated: "A sane future is not something distant or dependent upon the seizure of state power, but is essentially in our own hands. For Mondragon, that has meant a search for equilibrio; William Foote Whyte and Kathleen Foote Whyte called equilibrio the first of the basic guiding principles that pervade the life of cooperatives:

"In discussions of important decisions, the word *equilibrio* appears again and again as a justification for any action proposed. The basic idea is that life in the cooperative should *not* be carried on as if it were a zero sum game in which some win and some lose. There must be a balancing of interests and needs; we hear it said that technological imperatives must be balanced with social objectives and the financial needs of the firm must be balanced with the economic needs of the members."[19]

It Is Simple: Regional Cooperatives Can Join Together By Signing Contracts

We don't just need more jobs; we need real, sustainable livelihoods! Livelihood systems are defined as social economic systems that provide, a good way to make a living with comparable (or better) wages and benefits when compared to the private sector; a new way for families to afford home ownership early in life, job security, and a comfortable retirement in exchange for a lifetime of good work.

As described above, worker-owned cooperatives can be built in constellations that eventually form a regional economic system, connecting businesses by contract to each other and to other businesses far outside of the region. When these businesses achieve economic self-sufficiency on a regional basis, with independence from the current anti-family economic system, I choose to call them Constellations.

Supply and Demand Can Be More Controlled for Sustainability by Cooperatives

Constellations of cooperatives may be designed to have their own banks, manufacturing industries, construction industries, agricultural production, super markets and solar, wind, geothermal and hydrogen energy production. Alternative energy production will focus on the best available technologies. Renewable energy will be one of the largest exports, if not *the* largest export product that Constellations can sell in order to buy those luxury items which they cannot yet produce or choose not to produce. As existing small and medium sized businesses, and even some enlightened large businesses, adopt the Mondragon Style worker/owner guiding principles, with guaranteed bank loans to maintain and expand their businesses, they will thrive. When a regional Constellation of cooperatives reaches an established worker/owner population of 500,000 to one million, they will have reached control of supply and demand, in large measure, over the basic necessities of life, and therefore can control the prices of commodities produced and sold within the Constellation to their fellow worker/owners. *This is real economic power to the people!*

A Rural and City Partnership

There are many thriving cooperatives across the United States, with annual revenues of $175 billion. Land O' Lakes Butter, Ocean Spray, Ace Hardware and Publix Supermarkets, with 1,000 stores, are all large cooperatives. Land O' Lakes Butter is an old cooperative, based in Arden Hills, Minnesota. One can easily fill a grocery cart with quality products made by agricultural cooperatives. However, at this time, they do not have a Mondragon Style bank and they are not part of a Constellation. When cooperatives form contractual relationships together, be they rural or city, they can benefit greatly from purchasing each other's products.

For example, wise city chefs learned long ago that to obtain the highest quality and freshest produce they needed to go out to the countryside and make arrangements with local farmers. City restaurants and supermarkets can best be supplied locally, for quality and to cut down transportation costs. City governments, led by city planners, need to draw maps of the available rural farmland and protect it from further development for the long range good of their cities. There is usually enough land that is not good for farming to allow some expansion, but it should be held to a minimum, as in Portland, Oregon. Portland, the state's biggest city established an Urban Growth Boundary, a line on the map that wisely sets limits on development so that the farmer's land would not become sprawling tract housing.

E.J. Dionne Jr., a columnist for *The Washington Post,* describes this planning system that was put in place in 1973 as "shocking", because it won support from environmentalists *and* business people. Dionne wrote:

"Limiting urban sprawl has become something of a civic religion here and one of the city's selling points. When Republican Governor Tom McCall pushed the system in 1973— it covers the whole state—his major concern was for Oregon's natural environment."[20]

Concentrating growth within an "urban reserve" has changed the way Oregon cities develop. Houses are packed more tightly using single lot line zoning to give incentives to developers to build townhouses, using much less land. The boundary has been moved slightly to accommodate some growth, but it will survive because of the depth of public support. The planners have established a high level of citizen participation. Robert Landauer, former editor for *The Oregonian,* said: "It's built, created, fashioned and textured by the people who have to live with the results."

Metropolitan governments have authority to make decisions covering the entire region, which enables them to protect valuable farm land. At the same time Portland built a light rail system that has attracted development along the line even before that section of rail line was built. It is axiomatic that developers will jump at the chance to build commercial enterprises on public investment in public transportation. We will explore the power of this strategy in Part 5, focusing on building Satellite New Towns to replace urban sprawl, while enhancing job creation in renewable energy.

Regional Cooperatives Can Have More Control over Supply and Demand

If one crop or commodity fails, the Constellation will have already developed substitutes, through advanced, democratic and intelligent planning. But most importantly, worker owner cooperatives can control supply and demand pricing.

For example, let us assume that a large agribusiness can sell corn to people in a Constellation for 20 cents less than the cooperatives can produce it and send it to market. However, within the Constellation of cooperatives, they know that 500 hundred fellow cooperative workers will by jobless if they buy less expensive corn from the large agribusiness. Within the democratic workplace of the Constellation, they decide that the livelihoods of their fellow worker/owners are of far more value than paying 20 cents more for corn. They reject the large agribusiness offer and celebrate the solidarity and life-giving values of the Mondragon Style. At the regional level, a true Livelihood System can flourish and be sustained outside of "market forces", which always have the potential of being totally destructive to livelihoods.

Cooperatives will choose to maintain a *sustainable economic structure*, which has benefits for all, rather than a highly competitive economic system that is subject to the rise and fall of prices and the destruction of worker's livelihoods in order to have a larger profit margin, for the CEO and his or her lieutenants but not all of the workers.

Mondragon's Economic Ladder

There is a special cooperative in Mondragon that provides an economic ladder for young people, called Allecoop. Young people are given jobs to assemble electrical components, wiring modules for household appliances and electrical wiring for vehicles. These are tasks that the manufacturing cooperatives farm out to Allecoop and they pay enough to enable youths to work their way through college, while getting vocational training. This unique co-op factory is largely run by students.[20]

This brings to mind the stark fact that there is no complete economic ladder, as such, for most of the poor people in America, because too many rungs are missing. There are many fine high schools that offer various programs to attempt to fill this great void, yet they do not reach down into the ghettos. When, I researched this lack of an economic ladder in the City of West Palm Beach, I was told by school district officials "that some minority students refused to participate in their programs." While this may be true, that is where the outreach ended. That job was left for a handful of very dedicated non-profits, such as Urban Youth Impact, which provided centers where students could find a mixture of entertainment, lunches and incentives to find a career path. That is essentially what is offered in America—a career path, without the means to afford it. We need to pay counselors that can reach into the lives of young people. There are, as of yet, no manufacturing cooperatives like Mondragon's so that millions of young people in the United States could work part-time into a college education or vocational training. Far too much manufacturing has been set-up outside of America, thus greatly reducing such an opportunity to create student run industrial factories as in Allecoop. However, now there is a real demand in the United States for manufacturing to return to its former strength in the economy, as we address the coming energy crunch and re-building of the American economy. The basic concept of Allecoop is to provide an economic ladder for very young people. This concept can be developed and implemented by local governments with a public/private partnership primarily directed to young people who will often turn to crime, prostitution and drug trafficking if they are not given opportunities to earn money, while in high school.

There needs to be an organization, comparable to Allecoop that is available to allow young people, even in the eighth grade, to earn some pocket money and save some for college or vocational schools. Even if they only can work 6 hours per week, young people in the poorer neighborhoods need to have that small amount of pocket money to proudly take their girlfriends to a movie or buy a sundae, to show the drug lords that they can make it without resorting to drug pushing and prostitution.

Most importantly, the U.S. style Allecoop needs to be administered by the single parents in the neighborhood, or have them on the board of directors. Those single parents know who the bad guys are who are trying to lead their children into the bad paths. Those parents can also raise their voices in the larger community to ask for, and receive funds to operate their own Allecoop. Those parents care about their children and they can provide the vital networking to reach out to young people who have refused the standard school district career path, which is incomplete in terms of a guaranteed end path.

It costs an average of $30,000 per year to keep those young people, mostly caught in the drug trade, in prison. If the federal government set up an Allecoop style organization in the poorer neighborhoods, and let the very young start to earn $2,000 per year for five years, the government would save $20,000 per year for each young person whose life is not destroyed through petty drug crimes and prostitution. That young person could then go on to find his/her career path and pay as much as $99,000 (66 yrs. X $1,500) in federal taxes over their lifetime, instead of costing the government $30,000 times the number of years in prison. Therefore, it is bargain for the federal government to fund Allecoop-style organizations across the nation.

Transforming Existing Corporations

One may ask, "What about existing corporations? How does one expect them to change? At this writing, large corporations have a huge power structure that is now in control of almost all of the economy and the strongest lobbyist voices controlling most of Congress. How could one expect them to adopt a new cooperative corporate charter, provide for their employees and reduce their obscene upper management salaries?"

The answer is that cooperatives can simply let existing corporations do as they will. If we cannot change them into adopting truly good values, we certainly can build new worker-owned cooperation style businesses in thriving regions with

63

cooperative values and principles right beside the existing corporations. After a few years, or perhaps a decade, people will see the difference and many corporations will see that it is important to treat their employees much better or lose them to the Mondragon-Style cooperatives. The most enlightened corporations, even very large ones like those with the United Steel Workers, and the United Auto Workers, who collaborate with Mondragon, and small businesses, will be eager to join worker/owner cooperatives to benefit from the advantages that they offer.

Also, many existing businesses will be happy to act as suppliers to large and growing cooperatives. The coming boom in cooperative corporations will lead to the education of those suppliers about the joys, job security and good compensation of being a worker-owner. Sustainable employment and a guaranteed good retirement are very strong incentives, and powerful regional cooperatives can provide that retirement package as they have done for decades in Mondragon. All that worker-owned cooperatives have to do is sign them up with a beautiful, mutually appreciated agreement to have the vision, values and will to serve people and our lives gets a whole lot better.

2012: The Year of the Co-op!

United Nations Secretary-General Ban Ki-moon declared 2012 the Year of the Co-op. With the theme of "Cooperative

Enterprises Build a Better World", the UN is seeking to encourage the growth and establishment of cooperatives all over the world. A billion people are members of co-ops around the world. Over 100 million jobs are in cooperatives world-wide.

A New Definition of Wealth: Advancing Humankind's Forward Days

The capital of the Mondragon system is essentially community or worker owned capital, not capital simply owned or controlled by a few men or boards of directors, the cooperatives or the Mondragon bank itself. The various accounts and resources of the co-ops, is social capital in the sense of its social commitment: it is the working capital of the co-ops (retained earnings, personal internal-capital accounts, personal savings accounts, buildings, machinery, land), much of it voluntarily committed by individuals or by groups of cooperators. The accumulated wealth of the cooperators is "wealth" as Buckminster Fuller defined it: it is not a pile of money, but rather "wealth that will advance mankind's forward days and our children's forward days." The Mondragon Style bank is the organization that ensures that this wealth will be used democratically for the benefit of the regional socio-economic system.

This is voluntarism conditioned by the pursuit of *equilibrio* and inspired by a combination of idealism and enlightened self-interest. Its success is manifested not only in economic gains but in the unquantifiable, though palpable, social benefits of the operation of the bank and the cooperators. The Mondragon Cooperative Corporation is a true Livelihood System, providing a happier workplace with more sustainable financial security. This is a socio-economic foundation for nation building at home with Christ's values of Truth, Goodness, Justice and the pursuit of the common good.

Overcoming the Major Flaws in Capitalism

There are four major flaws in the Capitalist system that can be eliminated by establishing a national cooperative corporation economic system. These destructive flaws are (1) rampant uncontrolled greed; (2) the conflict between capital and labor and (3) the lack of long range planning to create new jobs, with major bank funding to sustain startups. Mondragon has overcome these three flaws by creating worker-owner enterprises and by putting a cap on salaries of general managers and bankers. Workers are also owners and they want to create new jobs for their offspring and for the community. (4) As Pope Francis wrote in *The Joy of the Gospel,* "No to a financial system which rules rather than serves." The world's richest 85 people have as much wealth as half of the world—3.5 billion people, according to a report by Oxfam, "Working for the Few".[21]

There are and will be many attempts to reform capitalism in an effort to maintain that system which is intrinsically corrupt because of these four major flaws. That is like putting lipstick on a poisonous snake. Until these four poisons are removed, it will always be able to come back and bite you. We need to replace the evil practices of corporations with a worker-owner structure in order to survive as a compassionate, cooperative society that does not destroy the planet, our only home, as today's corporations are well on their way to doing. We must stop them in their tracks before they kill all life on the planet with fossil fuel burning which has and will raise the temperature of the Earth until it is out of control. We cannot be that uncaring and pathological and still survive.

In Part 2, we will show how the oil crunch is rapidly becoming a given, and we will examine how the future threat of rising oil prices requires long range planning and how the rising cost of gasoline creates a powerful demand for nation building at home.

PART 2

THE OIL CRUNCH IS GUARANTEED

The Pentagon Leads the Way to Shift from Oil to Solar, Wind and Biofuels

The Pentagon has proclaimed that the military must be supplied by other energy sources than oil within the next 30 years, because *the price and availability of oil for the U.S. cannot be guaranteed 30 years hence.* These facts were published September 27, 2010, in a report from the Department of Defense to the military, titled *The Joint Operating Environment.*[1] This report is a long-range planning assessment of critical factors that will impact the operational capability of the military over the next 30 years. A second report, *Fueling the Future Force,*[2] by Christine Parthemore and John Nagl, was published on September 27, 2010, by the Center for a New American Security.

John Nagl wrote the book on counter-insurgency in Iraq, which indicates that this report has been widely read by President Obama and some policy makers.

The Military and the Domestic Economy Must Be Independent of Oil within 30 Years

This coming energy crunch sets the stage for the United States to transform itself in many very positive ways. There is a full blown global consciousness now that survival on the

68

planet, human safety and developing sustainable livelihood systems for families is far more dramatically critical than any military venture. The military planners have already concluded that the military itself must be completely independent of oil within 30 years. This point was constantly brought home in the *Fueling the Future Force* report. The report was done by a national security and defense think tank based in Washington, D.C. which has political connections to the White House, with several former employees being picked for key posts by the Obama administration. In fact, a 2009 opinion piece in the *Washington Post* stated that "In the era of Obama…the Center for a New American Security may emerge as Washington's go-to think tank on military affairs." As stated above, it is clear that the Obama administration is aware of these issues and should be developing a plan of action to transition from oil to solar, wind and biofuel energy sources. The *Fueling the Future Force* report stated the following, in powerful language:

"The U.S. Department of Defense (DOD) must prepare now to transition smoothly to a future in which it does not depend on petroleum. This is no small task: up to 77 percent of DOD's massive energy needs – and most aircraft, ground vehicles, ships and weapon systems that DOD is purchasing today – depend on petroleum fuel. Yet, while many of today's weapons and transportation systems are unlikely to change dramatically or be replaced for decades, the petroleum needed to operate DOD assets may not remain affordable, or even reliably available, for the lifespan of these systems.

To ready America's armed forces for tomorrow's challenges, DOD should ensure that it can operate all of its systems on non-petroleum fuels by 2040. This 30-year timeframe reflects market indicators pointing toward both higher demand for petroleum and increasing international competition to acquire it. Moreover, the geology and economics of producing petroleum will ensure that the market grows tight long before petroleum reserves are depleted. Some estimates indicate that the current global reserve-to-production (R/P) ratio – how fast the world will produce all currently known recoverable petroleum reserves at the current rate of production – is less than 50 years. Thus, given projected supply and demand, we cannot assume that oil will remain affordable or that supplies will be available to the United States reliably thirty years hence."[3]

The Department of Defense Is Installing Solar and Wind Power on US Bases

The DOD has developed a comprehensive and strategic **Master Energy Performance Plan** to comply with its own clean energy goals, executive orders and legislation, according to a report by the PEW Charitable Trust: "How the Department of Defense Leverages Private Resources to Enhance Energy Security and Save Money on U.S. Military Bases", published January 16, 2014. The report states: "For example, efficiency projects at military installations more than doubled to 1,339 from 630 and renewable energy projects at military bases increased by 54 percent to 700 in fiscal 2012 from 454 in fiscal 2010." Clearly, the leaders of the domestic economy should follow the lead of the military to avoid a future energy catastrophic shutdown.

Seeing a map of the countries with oil reserves to sell to the highest bidder enables the authors of "Fueling the Future Force" to present some stark geopolitical realizations:

"Ominously, many major suppliers to the United States could produce their current proved reserves in a fairly short time horizon if they continue at the present rate: for example, the R/P ratio for Canada (the top supplier to the United States in 2009, providing more than 20 percent of total oil imports) stands at about 28 years today. For the United States itself, it is 11 years. The only countries with current R/P ratios longer than 75 years are Venezuela, Iran, Iraq, Kuwait and the United Arab Emirates."[4]

Clearly, Venezuela, Iraq and Iran are not our most reliable oil sellers. The painful truth is that the United States has made enemies among this group and others, especially by supporting falling dictatorships in the Middle East. China, Asia and India are actively pursuing those same countries for their own long range supplies, while the U.S. carried on its warring occupations of sovereign states in the Middle East. Brazenly invading sovereign nations in the Middle East is not the way to make good friends among those who have oil to sell to the highest bidder and their most trusted allies. After invading Iraq and destroying its infrastructure with no justification, and then occupying that country for ten years, how many loyal allies does the United States have in the Middle East? Especially after the fall of Mubarack in Egypt, the U.S. is on thin ice. Meanwhile, the continuing conflicts in the Middle East centered on Israel and massive unemployment can burst into a major disruption that will cut off oil supplies for the U.S. from many Arab nations.

The International Energy Agency *World Energy Outlook* report of 2012

This report from the prestigious Paris-based organization claims that advances in drilling technology, will produce an upsurge in North American energy output. It predicted that the United States would overtake Saudi Arabia and Russia to become the planet's leading oil producer by 2020. This is partly true due to a *decline* in oil production by Saudi Arabia and Russia. At best, the global supply of oil is not going to grow appreciably, while global demand still grows. In the U.S. the prediction of the rise of domestic oil and gas production was met with great jubilation. However, the IEA report noted that "Much is riding on Iraq's success. Without this supply growth from Iraq, oil markets would be set for difficult times." China now has arranged access to 50% of Iraqi oil fields. We must remember that the U.S. is still an oil importing nation and oil prices (and gasoline prices) are set globally, no matter that we produce more oil for domestic consumption or sale.

Burning Fossil Fuels Is Burning the Planet

The IEA reported, "Taking all new developments and policies into account, the world is still failing to put the global energy system onto a more sustainable path." Indeed, this most shocking part of the report was totally ignored by the American national media. The IEA determined that even accounting for policy commitments already made or contemplated by world governments, CO_2 emissions are expected to rise precipitously over the next two decades, resulting in a global temperature increase of 3.6 degrees.

We are already seeing what 1.5 degrees can do, with Super Storm Sandy, the drastic drought in 60% of the nation, killing the corn crop and turning the Corn Belt into a dust bowl and the rise in sea level and storm surge. We do not want to see what a 2 degree increase can do, yet alone the devastation of 3.6 degrees. However, our so-called "corporate leaders" are barreling down that path, burning fossil fuels with jubilation as they worship money over the needs of the nation and the world.

China, India, Asia and all Parts of the World Demand Oil Also

It is not hard to grasp that the American public may not have seen this all coming down the road so fast. Most Americans may think that gas prices will go up a bit, but we will get by, as in the past. Well, no, gas prices will go up a bit in 2014, and up substantially more in 2015, when global *surplus* oil production capacity will entirely disappear, and go down even more in 2015, *when the global shortfall in output could reach nearly 10 million barrels a day, according to the DOD's "Joint Operating Environment" report.* What we have here is a situation where China now has the same demand for oil as the United States: importing 1.5 million barrels a day in 2013. China is buying one-half of all Iraqi oil and they accept Iraq's strict restrictions on profit. This is coupled with a surprisingly quick shortfall in global production, partially due to lack of enough engineers and drilling platforms and the lack of easy to reach oil.

Global Demand for Oil Has Skyrocketed in "Emerging Markets"

The overarching surprise is that China and India and the other "emerging countries" have grown at astonishing rates. Their peoples are eager to drive cars, and have many of the luxuries that have been long taken for granted in the U.S. In China, their economy has grown at 9% a year while the U.S. Gross Domestic Product (GDP) was dragging well behind in a deep recession. China, India, Asia and the rest of the "emerging nations" have been growing and consuming global oil supplies at such shocking rates, partly because U.S. corporations have given them U.S. technology in exchange for their fast growing markets. American international corporations have not only outsourced American jobs, their foreign investments have radically speeded up the consumption of oil by China, India and Asian countries. Ironically, American corporations are causing the deprivation of affordable oil supplies to their own nation, by shifting most of their investments to "emerging markets." This is happening primarily because of rampant and uncontrolled greed for more profit as the top priority in the capitalist system.

Billions of 401(K) Dollars Are Now Advised to Go to "Emerging Markets"?

American financial advisors are encouraging American workers to invest their retirement funds in these same "emerging markets", because they can often earn a higher return. But is our pursuit of making a bit more money on our investments, the highest value of American workers, especially if it substantially raises gasoline prices?

J. Michael Martin, chief investment officer of Financial Advantage, Inc., in Columbia, Md., said, "We live in a culture where we've built this debt that's going to slow us down, so you might as well diversify into the countries where the opportunity is very big." This quote was taken from an Associated Press article by David Pitt, "International markets diversify your 401 (k)."[5]

Therefore, the natural workings of the global economic system will encourage Americans to drive up demand for oil, globally, at an even faster pace. At this point in our history, the continued American investment abroad for larger profits only, has reached truly sociopathic levels. Large investment opportunities in renewable energy await us at home and they can enable corporations and investors to have enough profit, while serving the noble purpose of saving the nation. If this uncomprehending ignorance and greed is promoted and allowed to continue, Americans could be paying gasoline prices as high as $5.00 to $6.00 per gallon in perhaps five to ten years. This will make it all the harder to outrace the oil crisis by producing enough biofuels and electricity for bus transit and hydrogen/electric cars at home. However, many, if not most Americans have been brain-washed to believe that return on investment at the highest possible level is a sacred doctrine of capitalism that must be continued even if it means continuous and unsustainable increases in gas prices. Never mind that if this "highest profit" doctrine is maintained, it will inevitably lead to people not being able to afford gasoline to get to work, day care, school and shopping. Never mind that this could result in a collapse of the American economy with the loss of hundreds of thousands of jobs.

Jet Fuel is the Most Difficult to Produce

The Department of Defense report states that 56% of total demand by the military is used for jet fuel. Jet aircraft engines must have the high energy density that can only be provided by chemical fuels. Electricity does not give airplanes the immediate power boost needed to lift big jet planes off the runway.

Solar energy derived from non-food biofuels is one hope to fuel jet airplanes, yet scaling up that technology has not yet been achieved. During that endeavor it may well require sacrifices by scaling back the amount of jet fuel that is consumed by the Air Force and Navy jets, and a scaling back in the number of civilian jet flights made each day. The military is rapidly advancing the use of lighter drone aircraft to reduce the amount of airplanes required to accomplish some of their missions.

Towards Solutions: "Hacking" Photosynthesis

As described in the book, *Abundance*, by Peter Diamondis and Steven Kotler, the Department of Energy is pursuing another pathway to meet our fuel needs.

"The Agency is also interested in hacking photosynthesis. Secretary Chu's SunShot Initiative has now funded the Joint Center for Artificial Photosynthesis (JCAP), a $122 million multi-institution project being led by Caltech, Berkeley and Lawrence Livermore National Laboratory. JCAP's goal is to develop light absorbers, catalysts, molecular linkers, and separation membranes—all the necessary components for faux photosynthesis. "We're designing an artificial photosynthesis process," says Dr. Harry Atwater, director of Caltech Center for Sustainable Energy Research and one of the project's lead scientists. "By 'artificial' I mean there's no living or organic component in the whole system. We're basically turning sunlight, water, and CO2 into storable, transportable fuels—we call 'solar fuels'—to address the other two-thirds of our energy consumption needs that normal photovoltaics miss."[6]

Not only will these solar fuels be able to power our cars and heat our buildings, Atwater believes that he can increase the efficiency of photosynthesis tenfold, perhaps a hundredfold— meaning solar fuels could completely replace fossil fuels. We're approaching a critical tipping point," he says. "It is very likely that, in thirty years, people will be saying to each other, 'Goodness gracious, why did we ever set fire to hydrocarbons to create heat and energy?'"[7]

There are many companies involved in the research and production of bio-fuels. Exxon has partnered with Craig Venter's company, Synthetic Genomics, Inc. to reliably mass produce bio oils from algae. As reported in the book *Abundance*, Paul Roessler, who heads the project, summarized their work as follows:

"In theory, once perfected, we could run this process continuously and just harvest the oil. The cells just keep cranking it out. This way you don't have to harvest all of the cells, instead just scoop up the oils they excrete. Our goal is to get to 10,000 gallons per acre per year, and to get it to work robustly at the level of a two-square-mile facility.

To understand how ambitious Venter's goals are, let's do the math: two square miles is 1,280 acres. At 10,000 gallons of fuel per acre, that's 12.8 million gallons of fuel per year. Using today's average of twenty-five miles per gallon and 12 thousand miles driven per year, two square miles of algae farms produce enough fuel to power around 26,000 cars. So how many acres does it take to power America's entire fleet? With roughly 250 million automobiles in the United States today, that translates to about 18,750 square miles, or about 0.49 percent of the U.S. land area (or about 17 percent of Nevada)."[8]

Scaling up bio fuels just to meet car needs is clearly a huge task. Perhaps we should consider using bio fuels for aircraft and use hydrogen fuel cell and/or electricity to power cars. Let's examine the fuel needs of aircraft in order to clarify the whole picture of what it will take to replace oil.

Cooperation between the Military and Civilian Uses of Fuels Begins Soon

The Economist reported that "civil aviation is expected to use 250 billion liters of jet fuel in 2010".[9] Assuming such a consumption level, as the price of oil increases there will be real competition for biofuel between the military and the American flying public. The question looms large already: Will the Air Force reduce its consumption of jet fuel and/or will the nation's commercial airlines reduce the number of flights, or both? The Navy and Air Force plan to use a 50/50 mixture of biofuels with petroleum derived fuel (kerosene). Cellulosic ethanol costs at least $4.00 per gallon, according to Wallace

Tyner, an economist at Purdue University. As imported oil prices climb over the next 10 years to 20 years, certain Members of Congress may be faced with a choice: do I drive to Washington, D.C. for 14-36 hours, or do I vote to significantly reduce the U.S. warring domination of the globe by our military air power so that more Americans can afford to fly domestically? Clearly, the awesome scale of our fuel needs, the time required and the national effort has not been considered by the Members of Congress to date.

What will it be Members of Congress: endless draining of taxpayer dollars for war or shall we pursue global peace? At last, Congress will be shortly faced with decisions between war and peace. Choosing peace may become the easiest choice for the first time in their lives. If Congress continues to fund warring against the wishes of 63% of Americans, the public outcry will only rise in tandem with soaring gasoline prices. Unaffordable gas prices will mean that millions of suburbanites cannot get to work, shopping, school and day care. Congress needs to wake up to these facts now.

Global Competition for Oil Leaves the U.S. with Less Available Oil

The wars in Iraq and Afghanistan were all done under the policy of pursuing our "national interests". Well, no, it has not worked out that way. Instead, the Bush Administration has alienated much of the world against the United States, as witnessed by the huge demonstrations around the world just before the unjustified invasion of Iraq.

The *Fueling the Future Force* report shows a map that delivers a strong visual message that the last remaining oil, *that is easy to extract*, is in the hands of nations that are *not* our reliable allies. The U.S. has supported many of the dictators in the Middle East that are being thrown out of power. The new rulers may well be Islamists with a long memory of how the U.S. kept those dictators in power. They may well prefer to sell the last remaining oil to China, Asia, India and other less aggressive nations of the world.

The ten plus years of occupation in Afghanistan has also met fierce resistance by the Pashtun Tribes, who are 49 million strong, and live in Pakistan and Afghanistan. The Pashtun and their allies have driven out the British and the Russians from their homeland. *After all, it is their land.* The temporary blocking of the Kyber Pass by the Pakistani Pashtun backed up 6,500 American trucks, mostly with oil for the American military in Afghanistan, for a period of 11 days. This is just one clear example of how people who are unhappy with U.S. war policies can totally cut off military oil supply lines. Pakistan is protesting against U.S. drone attacks by blocking NATO supply lines.

The United States is no longer seen as a global "Peace Keeper", because of those clear acts of unilateral arrogance, dominant military power and decade long occupations. The

Iraq war was a premeditated act of killing, not merely "collateral damage". It has taken over 85,000 Iraqi *civilian* lives, mostly women and children, as of 2010, according to latest estimates, and two million civilians have been forced out of their homes to become refugees.

This aggressive unilateral assault to secure the United States oil supply has backfired. Developing the oil fields in Iraq has been set back because of the massive bombing and destruction of that nation's infrastructure, water and electricity supplies. It is now seen as a failure, because even if Iraq can produce 13 million barrels a day, global competition for oil will continue to raise prices faster than the available supply. Having destroyed Iraq's infrastructure, obtaining a sufficient amount of Iraqi oil to supply the U.S. will be delayed for 20 years, according to Fatih Birol, the International Energy Agency's chief economist. The oil that will come on line for the U.S. will likely be too little too late. Also, the China National Petroleum Company has an oil contract in the al-Ahdab oil field in Iraq. Most importantly, China can afford to pay more for oil than the United States and China does not require Congressional approval to pay more. Iraqi oil will go to the highest bidder who agrees to their requirements regarding profit in the production of that oil. *The Joint Operating Environment* report's main concern is not fueling the U.S. military machine so much as *funding* it: "Another potential effect of an energy crunch could be a prolonged U.S. recession which could lead to deep cuts in defense spending as happened during the Great Depression." Most importantly, the U.S. has spent so much on these wars and the total military industrial complex budget that America is on the verge of bankruptcy. Clearly, bankruptcy from unnecessary military expenditures is not in our "national interests". According to Roger Stern, a Princeton economist, it has cost the United States $8 trillion dollars to provide military security in the Gulf since 1976. That's Trillion with a "T".

The Real "National Interest" Is Producing Hydrogen Fuel Cell Cars and Electricity from Solar and Wind with Hydrogen Fuel Cell Storage

The endless requests for more war funding is justified by what the politicians call America's "national interests." This evasion of reality by the politicians and corporations will now come to the foreground of the debate on what constitutes the "national interests." After all, the military is not the only group that will be powerfully affected by the coming energy crunch: the American people who have been forced by suburban sprawl to buy cars and fuel to get to work and earn a living will be threatened to survive.

Table 1. Cost of Gasoline per gallon in Europe and the United States

United States	$3.25 to 3.90
EU Average	$7.61
Sweden	$8.46
Italy	$9.02
Denmark	$8.95
Germany	$8.12
United Kingdom	$8.71

Source: International Business Times
April 20, 2013

In April 2011, gasoline prices reached $3.79 per gallon in the U.S. In a poll by the Associated Press-GfK, two-thirds of those polled said that gas cost spikes will cause serious financial hardship. When fuel costs reach even $5.00 to $6.00 per gallon, the American public will desperately want affordable hydrogen fuel cell cars and strong government leadership to supply biofuels rather than petroleum. In the north, heating oil must be replaced by solar and wind electrical power and in the south, solar and wind electrical energy must be available for air conditioning. *The Joint Operating Environment* also stated: "reduction of economic output based on Peak Oil might affect market-driven economies in a way that they stop functioning altogether, leaving the possibility of a relatively steady downward trajectory."

The authors of these long-range planning military reports are free to say the truth. Military planners are not obligated to "the financial elite", corporations, the administration or Congress. In fact, it is their job to plan for the future of the military and speak truth to the generals and admirals with an open mind.

Why the Oil Crisis Is Guaranteed to Happen

Here is a classic example of American business insanity: American and other international companies are rapidly creating a huge, global demand for oil in "emerging markets", including China, India and Asia. This demand level has caught the U.S. leaders and military by surprise. Our own American companies, in order to make larger profits abroad are driving up the very oil demand that guarantees the coming oil crisis in America. It is not a matter of if: it is a matter of time. The surge in oil and natural gas production in the U.S. will buy some time, perhaps even 10 years, but the endgame is clear.

The Economic Growth Model Based on Oil Is Stalling Out

Jeremy Rifkin underscores the problem with rising economic growth, based on oil, as follows: "When the price of oil passed the $100 per barrel mark, something unthinkable just a few years earlier, spontaneous protests and riots broke out in twenty-two countries because the steep rise in the price of cereal grains—tortilla protests in Mexico and rice riots in Asia. The fear of widespread political unrest sparked a global discussion around the oil-food connection. With 40% of the human race living on $2 per day or less, even a marginal shift in the price of staples could mean widespread peril. By 2008, the price of soybeans and barley had doubled, wheat had almost tripled, and rice had quintupled."[10] The United Nations Food and Agriculture Organization (FAO) reported that a record one billion human beings were going to bed hungry.

The fear spread as middle class consumers in the developed countries began to be affected by the steep oil price rise. The price of basic items in stores shot up. Gasoline and electricity prices soared. So did the price of construction materials, pharmaceutical products and packaging materials—the list was endless. By late spring, prices were becoming prohibitive and purchasing power began plummeting around the world. In July of 2008, the global economy shut down. That was the great economic earthquake that signaled the beginning of the end of the fossil fuel era."

Rifkin observed: "If aggregate economic output throttles (up) again at the same rate as it did in the first eight years of the twentieth century---which is exactly what is happening--- the price of oil will quickly rebound to $150 per barrel or more, forcing a steep rise in prices for all other goods and services, and will lead to another plunge in purchasing power and the collapse of the global economy." In other words, each new effort to regain the economic growth of the past will stall out at around $147 per barrel. This wild gyration between growth and collapse is the endgame. Economic growth cannot be based on oil, which is clearly a sun-setting energy supply.

"While speculators may have added fuel to the fire, the incontrovertible fact is for the past several decades we have been consuming three and a half barrels of oil for every new barrel we find. This reality is what determines our present condition and future prospects."[11]

When transportation costs reach high levels they are added to all goods and most services. When people and businesses cannot afford this price, the whole economy shuts down. People stop buying oil-based products and the price of oil goes down. As consumption builds back up to the 147 dollar a barrel level, the economy shuts down again. This is the endgame that Rifkin described. Clearly, the goal of having a "growing economy", based on oil and coal energy, cannot be sustained. We must shift to renewable energy as quickly as possible. Delay is not an option, as we shall see.

The Era of "Easy Oil" Is Nearly Gone: Hard to Get Oil Costs Much More and Way too Much Carbon Dioxide Will Be Released into the Atmosphere and Oceans

The International Energy Agency (IEA), a Paris-based organization that governments rely on for their energy information and forecasts, may have put the issue of global peak oil production to rest in its "2010 World Energy Outlook" report. According to the IEA, global peak production of crude oil probably occurred in 2006 at seventy million barrels per day. The report stunned the international oil community and caused deep dread among global businesses whose life line is crude oil.

The International Energy Agency examined the long term yields of the world's largest producing oil fields which contains the "easy oil" that supplies the bulk of the world's energy. The results were stunning: those fields are expected to lose 75% of their productive capacity over the next 25 years, which will eliminate 52 million barrels per day from the oil supplied to the whole world. This means that we either find new oil to replace those 52 million barrels or we need to shift to renewable energy resources.

Michael T. Klare is a professor of peace and world security studies at Hampshire College and has published *The Race for What's Left: The Global Scramble for the World's Last Resources.* His article, "A Tough-Oil World", posted on Huffington Post, 3-13-2012, provides a brief but stunning analysis of the huge reserves of hard to get oil around the globe. Klare wrote:

"Those who claim that the Petroleum Age is far from over often point to these reserves as evidence that the world can still draw on immense supplies of untapped fossil fuels. And it is certainly conceivable that, with the application of advanced technologies and a total indifference to environmental consequences, these resources will indeed be harvested. But easy oil it is not."[12]

Canada's Tar Sands and the Keystone XL Pipeline

Michael T. Klare described what "tough oil" involves as follows: "Until now, Canada's tar sands have been obtained through a process akin to strip mining, utilizing monster shovels to pry a mixture of sand and bitumen out of the ground. But most of the near-surface bitumen in the tar-sands-rich Alberta has now been exhausted, which means all future extraction will require a far more complex and costly process. Steam will have to be injected into deeper concentrations to melt the bitumen and allow its recovery by massive pumps. This requires a colossal investment of infrastructure and energy, as well as the construction of treatment facilities for all the resulting toxic wastes. According to the Canadian Energy Research Institute, the full development of Alberta's oil sands would require a minimum investment of $218 billion over the next 25 years, not including the cost of building pipelines to the United States (such as the proposed Keystone XL) for processing in U.S. refineries.

Tough oil reserves like these may provide most of the world's new oil in the years ahead. One thing is clear: even if they can replace easy oil in our lives, the cost of everything oil-related—whether the gas at the pump, in oil-based products, in fertilizers, in just about every nook and cranny of our lives – is going to rise in price. Get used to it. If things proceed as presently planned, we will be in hock to big oil for decades to come. This is the catastrophe of the century, if we are so weak and blind as to let it happen.

And don't forget the final cost: If all these barrels of oil and oil-like substances are truly produced from the least inviting places on this planet, then for decades to come we will continue to massively burn fossil fuels, creating ever more greenhouse gases as if there were no tomorrow. And here is the sad truth: if we proceed down the tough-oil path instead of investing massively in alternative energies, we may foreclose any hope of averting the most catastrophic consequences of a hotter and more turbulent planet. So, yes there is oil out there. But no, it won't be cheaper, no matter how much there is. And yes, the oil companies can get it, but looked at realistically, who would want it?" [12]

Here is another perspective on why we must take action now: Thomas Friedman, a columnist for the *New York Times,* declared in a recent article "Planet Earth is Full". Mr. Friedman cited the work of Paul Gilding, an Australian environmentalist-entrepreneur who has described our crisis in his book, *The Great Disruption: Why Climate Change Will Bring on the End of Shopping and the Birth of a New World.* Mr. Gilding first cites the work of the Global Footprint Network, an alliance of scientists, which has concluded that right now, global growth is using about 1.5 Earths because we are growing at a rate that is using up the Earth's resources far faster than they can be sustainably replenished. We are eating into our future even now. But Mr. Gilding is an optimist. As the impact of the Great Disruption hits us, he said, "Our response will be proportionally dramatic, mobilizing as we do in war. We will change at a scale and speed we can barely imagine today, completely transforming the economy, including our energy and transport industries, in just a few short decades."[13]

We Need to Give Government Leaders the Courage to Act

The Administration is aware of the urgent need to advance a new National Energy and Transportation Plan to transition from oil to renewable energy sources by 2040 in order to avoid the dire consequences of economic collapse. When the 1973 oil crisis hit, people took to the streets because they wanted cheap gasoline and they wanted the government to make sure that they would have gas to get to work, school and shopping. We do have the time now, in theory, of three to four decades to accomplish the daunting tasks ahead, however delay is not an option. The government and the media will need to give the population awareness that a global energy crisis is rapidly approaching and make long range plans in order to assure the public that we can meet the challenge. Today, we are sleep-walking and finding it very difficult to process these new realities. The famous psychologist Carl Jung remarked: "People cannot stand too much reality." However, the pressure of total economic collapse could even wake up Congress.

The "easy oil" economy has made it so easy for Americans to believe that the time for accelerated action can be pushed into the future. To make a sustainable transition from fossil fuels to renewable energies requires a large amount of affordable fossil fuels from which to work and more than one generation of time.

Alex Kuhlman, in his 2006 article,"Peak oil and the collapse of commercial aviation", states the case well:

"Today's market mechanisms are incapable of taking into account the long lead times and resources required to balance supply and demand, and ultimately replace fossil fuels. With oil production declining in almost every nation outside of the Middle East, and spare capacity already quickly disappearing throughout the system, the phenomena of peak oil itself and a pending decline is almost self-evident and hardly needs defending. While the potential apocalyptic implications are far more difficult to digest, they cannot be wished away.

Optimists may argue that technology, the market, brilliant scientists, and comprehensive government programs are going to hold things together. However, with an acute lack of awareness, time, knowledge, capital, energy and political will, it is impossible to see how we can continue with business as usual.

A new path must be chosen to conserve the underlying fossil fuel base required to develop and implement sustainable energy sources capable of running even a substantial fraction of countries such as the USA. Otherwise, we may lack the tools to move forward to replace a fluid so cheap, abundant and versatile."[14]

We cannot wait for a price signal of $133 per barrel of oil to awaken the public, media and government. The Peak Oil alarm clock has already sounded and it is time for long range planning in business as the military is doing now.

We can conclude from these reports that the production of solar and wind energy, electric/hydrogen cars, biofuels and hydrogen fuel cells for the general functioning of the American economy, yet alone the military, is now a necessity and must be in place over the next 30 years. We have a lethal emergency more threatening than war to America: the potential loss of our livelihoods, because we will not be able to get to work, day care, shopping and schools in gasoline driven cars. It will take another "Great Generation" to accomplish this transition to renewable energies and it will require cooperation on a grand scale, rather than destructive competition. We are truly challenged to undertake nation building at home as never before.

In Part 3, we will show how Germany is implementing a plan to lead the European Union into a carbon free future.

93

PART 3

SOLUTIONS: GERMANY LEADS THE WAY TO ELIMINATE CO2 AND BUILD A NEW GLOBAL ECONOMY

Jeremy Rifkin, author of *The Third Industrial Revolution: How Lateral Power Will Transform Society,* has written an excellent description of Germany's plan to regrow the global economy based on renewable energy, as follows:[1]

"While the rest of the world is in a near panic over the prospect of a second collapse of the global economy, a fresh new economic wind is blowing across Germany. In discussions with German business leaders over the past several months, and in recent conversations with Angela Merkel and key political leaders in Berlin, it has become clear that Germany is embarking on a journey into a new economic era.

Today, the distributed Internet communication revolution is converging with distributed renewable energies, giving birth to a powerful Third Industrial Revolution that is going to fundamentally change German Society.

The Merkel administration has launched an ambitious effort to transition the West's leading exporter into a Third Industrial Revolution (TIR). The federal government has teamed up with six regions across Germany to test the introduction of an "energy Internet" that will allow tens of thousands of German businesses and millions of home owners to collect renewable energies onsite, store them, partially in the form of hydrogen, and share green electricity across Germany in a smart utility network, just like we now share information online. Entire communities are in the process of transforming their commercial and residential buildings into green micro-power plants, and companies like Siemens and Bosch are creating sophisticated new IT software, hardware, and appliances that will merge distributed Internet communications with distributed energy to create the smart buildings, infrastructure and cities of the future."[2]

This new German industrial revolution is gaining momentum rapidly with the following events advancing toward a 40 year buildout:

The German government announced in May, 2011 that they would shut down the nation's 17 nuclear power plants by 2022 as Germany leads the world toward a carbon free and clean energy system. The German utility companies reported that renewable energy now accounts for 20% of the country's electricity, putting Germany ahead of schedule to produce 35% of its electricity from green sources by 2022.

On September 12, 20011, Dr. Dieter Zetsche, the Chairman of Daimler, unveiled the company's hydrogen fuel cell car at the opening of the Frankfurt International Auto Show. (For a pictorial review of the Daimler fuel cell power train, visit Daimler.com/Fuel Cell Drive Technology.)

"Daimler has joined with seven industrial partners – EnBW, Linde, OMV, Shell, Total, Vattenfall, and the National Organization of Hydrogen and Fuel Cell Technology – to establish hydrogen fueling stations across Germany in preparation for the mass production of zero emission fuel cell vehicles in 2015, setting the plan in motion for the beginning of the post-carbon auto era and the Third Industrial Revolution."[3] "The key is creating a seamless green energy infrastructure, electricity grid, and communication and transport network that will allow one billion people to engage in "sustainable" commerce and trade across the European continent and its periphery. This represents the next stage of European integration as a political union."[4]

"Even homeowners can now turn their houses into mini-power plants. A homeowner can install solar panels on his or her roof and generate enough electricity to power much or all of the home. Any surplus can be sold back to the grid, and payback on the solar installation costs can run anywhere from four to ten years."[5]

Rifkin proposes "green mortgages" to encourage more homeowners to finance their mini-power plants. As fuel cell and solar kits become less expensive, homes can produce energy and join the continental electric grid. The vision and plan adopted by the European Union is as follows:

The Five Pillars of the Third Industrial Revolution

"Like every other communication and energy infrastructure in history, the various pillars of a Third Industrial Revolution must be laid down simultaneously or the foundation will not hold. That's because each pillar can only function in relation to the others. The five pillars of the Third Industrial Revolution are (1) shifting to renewable energy; (2) transforming the building stock of every continent into micro-power plants to collect renewable energies on site: (3) deploying hydrogen and other storage technologies in every building and throughout the infrastructure to store intermittent energies; (4) using Internet technology to transform the power grid of every continent into an energy-shared intergrid that acts just like the Internet (when millions of buildings are generating a small amount of energy locally, on site, they can sell surplus back to the grid and share electricity with their continental neighbors); (5) transitioning the transport fleet to electric plug-in and fuel cell vehicles that can buy and sell electricity on a smart, continental, interactive grid."[6]

Rifkin shows the economic power of this social and industrial revolution as follows:

"The opportunity is clear. The European Union has 500 million consumers and an additional 500 million potential consumers in its partnership regions, giving it the prospect of becoming the largest and wealthiest internal commercial market in the world. The key is creating a seamless green energy infrastructure, electricity grid, and communication and transport network that will allow one billion people to engage in "sustainable" commerce and trade across the European continent and its periphery. This represents the next stage of European integration as a political union."[7]

In May 2007, the European Parliament issued a formal written declaration endorsing the Third Industrial Revolution (TIR) vision as the long-term economic road map for the European Union.

Rifkin has found that, thus far, American utility companies, for the most part, are reticent about introducing the TIR business model in the U.S. "There is a lot involved in the weighty decision to build two different smart grids—a centralized, top down system in the United States and a distributed and collaborative system in the European Union. Industry observers estimate that it will cost approximately $1.5 trillion between 2010 and 2030 to transform the existing U.S. power grid into an intelligent utility network. If the smart grid is unidirectional rather than bidirectional in design, the United States will have lost the opportunity to join with Europe in the Third Industrial Revolution and, with it, the prospect of retaining its leadership in the global economy."[8]

Rifkin favors a cooperative business model at the neighborhood nodal sites. Neighborhoods can create energy cooperatives to allow small micro-producers of energy to aggregate their capital and spread their risks so they can become effective players in the distributed energy market. "Recall that the creation of rural electric cooperative associations across the rural regions of the United States in the 1930's, 1940's, and 1950's brought electricity to millions of homes and small businesses, and is an example of the power inherent in the cooperative model. Because the Third Industrial Revolution communication/energy system is by nature a distributed and collaborative process, it favors the cooperative business model at the nodal sites."[9]

Rural Electric Power Cooperatives Already Exist in 47 States

Electric power cooperatives were created as one of President Franklin Roosevelt's New Deal programs. "The Rise of the Power Co-op Movement," by Brendan Smith and Jeremy Brecher, an article published by Commondreams.org, details just how strong these electric cooperatives have become:

"Today, America's 930 electric cooperatives are the sole source of electricity for 42 million people in 47 states – nearly 12 percent of the nation's population. They control $100 billion in assets and $31 billion in member equity."[10]

In many regions, these electric cooperatives can be used as a starting base for the development of several New Towns in groupings called Constellations, providing solar and wind energy, onsite and in buildings, which can be loaded onto a smart grid. This is also a powerful base for the development of worker/owner cooperatives, across the United States.

Alternatively, large scale solar-thermal power plants and wind power farm installations can become the center of brand new Constellations, in a region where there are several hundred small businesses, which would like to become worker/owner cooperatives, Mondragon Style. Bio-fuel energy production complexes are other centers on which Constellations can be built. Energy production for use in the Constellations is a necessity for self-sufficiency. Since the Constellations will want major exports, of up to 25% or more of their production so they can buy things not produced by them, it is very logical to generate more electricity as a major export item to regions with less sunlight and renewable resources.

There are two different approaches to energy production and distribution in the United States:

(1) One plan is to build the installation of giant solar farms in the southwest and giant wind farms in the Midwest and pass legislation that would mandate a high voltage direct current grid to transfer that electric power to the densely populated north and eastern regions. This is a centralized, top down model controlled by the major utilities.

(2) A second plan would be to implement the Third Industrial Revolution (TIR) model as described above that Germany is putting in place. This is a distributed lateral model, which would enable every home, business or factory to produce its own electricity and use a smart grid that will enable everyone to use solar and wind with hydrogen fuel cell storage.

The centralized approach has *not* been well received by the eastern governors and power companies, according to Jeremy Rifkin: "In July of 2010, eleven New England and mid-Atlantic governors sent a letter to the U.S. Senate majority leader, Harry

Reid, and the minority leader, Mitch McConnell, opposing a national electric transmission policy. The governors argued that centralizing wind and solar power in the western region of the country "would harm local regional efforts to promote local renewable energy generation…and hamper efforts to create clean energy jobs in our states." The question is whether renewable energy production will be centralized in one part of the country and distributed to the rest of the United States or generated locally everywhere and shared across the continent."[11]

"If, however, the federal government were to install a distributed national power grid that connects the entire continent and allows every local producer to feed electricity into the network, it would create the kind of lateral scaling that we've seen with distributed Internet business. The price of electricity would continue to drop as it did in the case of sharing information."[12]

The technology to accomplish this would rest with the creation of millions of household mini-power plants using hydrogen fuel cells as the "battery" storage device while using onsite solar, wind, and geothermal in the production of electricity.

Hydrogen Can Be Extracted From Seawater on a Global Basis

Purdue Professor of computer and electrical engineering, Jerry Woodall, and university scientists have developed a new method to extract hydrogen straight from seawater. The splitting hydrogen from water involves aluminum. Woodall says, "Since aluminum is low-cost, abundant…this technology can be used on a global basis and could greatly reduce the consumption of fossil fuels."[13] As this new TIR German economic model advances to usher in carbon-free electricity and transportation and a new path for job creation and residential participation in the production and distribution of energy, the world community will be watching to see if this new economic model can work for their continental market while dealing with the rising price of oil and the elimination of CO2. As they say in poker parlance, Germany is "ALL IN", placing its bets on hydrogen-electric cars and a hydrogen/solar, wind and geothermal electricity grid. The health of the biosphere cannot wait much longer than a 40 year buildout to end carbon emissions and 40 years is the target for the German buildout. However, America lags behind with lack of vision and political will.

Wind Power and Solar Power Are Now the Lowest Cost Energy Sources

Wind power at $0.07 per kilowatt hour is the lowest cost electric energy source. Solar thermal electricity costs about $0.11 per KWH. The average residential cost in the U.S. is 12 cents per KWH in 2014.

Once wind turbines and electric plants are built, *the fuel is free!* No expensive drilling and hauling is required as the Sun and wind provide the fuel. Most importantly they do not send massive amounts of CO_2 into the atmosphere. Solar and wind power are no longer "alternative energies": they are clearly the lowest cost energies based on full cost pricing, including climate change damages.

Researchers at Stanford University and the University of Delaware ran a computer model and discovered that wind power alone could meet all of our electricity needs. We can install wind turbines off shore and inland with large concentrations and they can be spaced so as not to affect each other. The new paper contradicts two earlier studies that said wind potential falls short of the goal of saturation because each turbine steals too much wind from other turbines. The new computer model Jacobson and Archer devised, separated winds in the atmosphere into hypothetical boxes stacked atop and beside one another. Each box has its own wind speed and weather. Thus, they exposed individual turbines to winds from several boxes at once, a degree of resolution unmatched by earlier models. Each turbine can reduce the amount of energy available to others. However, to reach saturation wind power potential, they report, the reduction only becomes significant when large numbers of turbines are installed, "many more than would ever be needed."

"We're not saying put turbines everywhere, but we have shown that there is no fundamental barrier to obtaining half or even several times the world's all-purpose power from wind by

2030. The potential is there, if we can build enough turbines," said Jacobson.

When the wind doesn't blow, hydrogen fuel cells can store energy and convert it back to electricity to power the nation. Even better, the wind is blowing somewhere all of the time. Electricity can be transported 2,400 miles with Direct Current transmission, with only a 15% maximum power loss. The report is "Saturation Wind Power Potential and its Implications for Wind Energy", Proceedings of the *National Academy of Sciences, 2012.* The authors are Mark Z. Jacobson and Cristina L. Archer.[14]

Capitalist investors always claim that we must choose the lowest price option. Logically, investors will be flocking to produce low cost solar and wind power. The only thing that can be holding them back are Crony Capitalists who have invested too much in coal, oil and "fracking" for natural gas, which all emit CO2. They are doing everything in their power to influence politicians in order to keep their oil, gas and coal Cash Cows regardless of the obvious damages they are causing across the nation with climate change.

We need to place a tax directly on carbon emissions to prevent continuing crop damage and billions in property damage from climate change. This means the Administration and Congress must look after the needs of the nation rather than continuing a cozy money flowing relationship with the Crony Capitalists and their 600 lobbyists working to buy legislation that favors CO2 emissions. Time has already run out for CO2 emitting industries. These emissions are much too expensive and lethal to plants, animals, life in the ocean, seafood and humans. Globally, nations cannot afford coal, oil and natural gas energies which are causing an uncomprehending march to extinction.

Lobbyists for large utility companies want the federal government to provide financing for large-scale projects so they can keep centralized control of the production of electricity. However, as Germany is showing, the nation needs to move rapidly to install small-scale solar on rooftops, parking lots, and businesses because of its huge potential. The large utilities can still keep their jobs by providing the intelligent grid system that will enable households and cooperative neighborhoods to finance and produce electricity with any surplus being sold back to the grid. Germany is on a path to provide 35% of its electricity from renewables by 2022. The United States needs to adopt this program as rapidly as possible to reduce the damage from climate change.

The World's Largest Investors, with $22.5 Trillion, Call for Climate Change Action

Singapore, November 20, 2012 (Reuters) – "A coalition of the world's largest investors called on governments to ramp up action on climate change and boost clean-energy investment or risk trillions of dollars in investment disruption to economies."[15]

In an open letter, the alliance of institutional investors, responsible for managing *22.5 trillion in assets,* said, rising greenhouse gas emissions and more extreme weather were increasing investment risks globally. The group called for dialogue between investors and governments to overhaul climate and energy policies. Current policies are insufficient to avert serious and dangerous impacts from climate change, said the group of investors from the United States, Europe, Asia and Australia.

The investments and retirement savings of millions of people were being jeopardized because governments were delaying emission cuts or more generous support of green energy. The group said the right policies would prompt institutional investors to invest in clean energy and efficiency, citing existing policies that have unleashed billions of dollars of renewable energy investment in China, the United Kingdom and Europe.

The World Bank said current climate policies meant that the world was heading for a warming of 4 degrees Celsius by 2100. That would trigger deadly heat waves and droughts, cut food stocks and drive up sea levels, which would flood most coastal areas, as recently demonstrated by Superstorm Sandy in New York and New Jersey, at a cost of $60 billion to the region.

The Hydrogen Age

Goeffrey B. Holland and James J. Provenzano have provided a detailed description of the technology and advantages of hydrogen in their book, *The Hydrogen Age: Empowering a Clean Energy Future*. They write: "This kind of vision applies to countries all over the world. Hydrogen, especially when made from renewable sources of energy like wind, solar, wave energy, tidal energy, hydro dams, or biomass, is a splendid way to store and deliver energy. It does not discriminate. Every country, every region, every town or village has some form of renewable energy close at hand that can be harnessed to produce the electric power needed to make hydrogen. Unlike all fuels that have come before, access to hydrogen cannot be controlled or restricted. In coming decades, this will liberate people in ways we can only begin to imagine. We stand on the cusp of the most important energy transition of all time. We are moving into *The Hydrogen Age*."[16]

Hydrogen Fuel Cell Cars Are Overtaking Electric Autos

The auto industry is already looking at hydrogen powered cars as a way to provide clean energy and outrun the coming fuel price crunch. Commitments by automobile manufacturers to develop hydrogen fuel cell cars have surged in recent months. Daimler, Toyota, Honda and Hyundai announced plans to build vehicles that use the most abundant element in the universe and emit only water vapor. Auto makers cite three main advantages of hydrogen fuel cell vehicles over electric powered vehicles.

(1) A fuel cell powered car can travel much longer distances than battery powered vehicles before needing to be refueled.

(2) Fuel cells can also be used in trucks, instead of natural gas.

(3) It takes only a few minutes to fill a tank with hydrogen or install a new fuel cell component.

As noted above, Daimler has begun to build a system of hydrogen re-fueling stations across Germany, to be ready to match a major surge of the production of hydrogen powered vehicles in 2015. Denmark and South Korea have plans to roll out dozens of stations in coming years.

Analysts estimate that such re-fueling stations can cost up to $1 million each to build. However, the threat of the rising cost of gasoline, which can paralyze the nation clearly shows this endeavor to be an economic and life giving bargain.

While the fuel cell Hyundai ix35 production cost is confidential, an executive said the target sale price for the next three to five years is $50,000. As mass production scales up that cost will come down to more affordable levels.

The relative high purchase price of today's electric cars comes from the cost of lithium-ion batteries, which a Ford executive recently revealed can amount to one-third of a car's price.[17]

The Final Energy Solution: It Comes From Sun, Wind Power and Hydrogen

R. Buckminster Fuller gave us the final solution in 1969, in his ground-breaking book, *Operating Manual for the Spaceship Earth:*

"I must observe also that we're not going to sustain life at all except by our successful impoundment of more of the Sun's radiant energy aboard our spaceship than we are losing. Quite clearly we have vast amounts of income wealth as Sun radiation.

Wherefore living only on our energy savings by burning fossil fuels which took billions of years to impound from the Sun or living on our capital by burning up our Earth's atoms is lethally ignorant and also utterly irresponsible to our coming generations and their forward days. If we do not comprehend and realize our potential ability to support all life forever we are cosmically bankrupt."[18]

Fuller's long range planning insights in his book, *Operating Manual for the Spaceship Earth* are more powerful today, 40 plus years later, which attests to the depth of his genius and forward-seeing vision. After 40 years of largely ignoring Bucky's genius-level advice, we are playing catch up, when we should be focusing powerfully on the final energy solution: the Sun's gift to humankind, which is also the Final Solution to bring abundance and peace on the Spaceship Earth.

In the United States, our short range vision has led to oil addiction and urban sprawl, which will demand hydrogen/ electric cars and rapid transit systems in order just to get to work and have a livelihood, as the cost of petroleum gets more and more expensive. The massive destruction from global warming and climate change has already cost $510 billion since the 1980's, not including the $60 billion impact of superstorm Sandy. This is a wake-up call that 80% Americans have finally seen, according to a recent poll. Seeing is believing, as the most basic skeptics say. Winter snow and ice storms have become much harsher in the Midwest and Northeast, resulting from climate change which caused a huge southern shift in the Jet Stream.

Long range energy planning and rapid implementation by corporations and government must replace short range blindness. We will now proceed to look at some of the current achievements in our efforts to impound the Sun's radiation to produce electric energy.

Solar Thermal Electric Power Plants

Solar Thermal Power, with hydrogen storage, as required, is one of the leading choices at this time because of its reliability and its smaller use of water, which has become scarce in many regions. Solar Thermal Power can also be used for de-salinization, which has already become necessary to meet water needs in many regions of the world. Make no mistake, the demand for water has already reached shortage levels in 10 major U.S. cities and also in other places around the world. We will need to fund de-salinization plants in many parts of the world.

At this writing, Solar Thermal power has good prospects, as it generates heat and does not require rare earth metals. Solar Thermal uses "concentrating solar thermal technology" in which mirrors concentrate sunlight on a boiler to produce heat. The heat is then used to produce steam, which drives highly efficient turbines to generate electricity. Here we are in the 21st century using steam power again! However, the energy to drive that process comes from the Sun, not from coal or other fossil fuels, which also came from the Sun, but were given to humankind as a precious safety factor until we learned to use the Sun's radiation directly for the generation of energy.

In 2009, BrightSource Energy, based in California, has signed the world's two largest business contracts to build a series of 14 solar thermal power plants that will collectively supply more than 2.6 gigawatts of electricity, which is enough to serve about 1.8 million new homes. *The Economist* magazine called solar thermal "The other kind of solar power".[19]

Solar thermal plants are typically built on a large scale. Solar thermal power plants have the following advantages: (1) they work best when it is hottest and demand is greatest. (2) The heat can be stored allowing the electricity to be available at all times. (3) Their turbine generators can be supplemented with hydrogen or biogas boilers to inexpensively add drive to them with more steam, enabling them to perform as reliably as a fossil fueled power plant. (4) It dramatically reduces carbon dioxide. (5) Dry-cooling can replace water-cooling using Stirling engines. This is very important in areas where there is a water shortage. (6) Steam generated from solar thermal collectors can help drive the turbines at existing coal and natural gas plants, thus reducing fuel costs and CO_2 emissions, until they can be totally replaced with 100% solar thermal, wind power and hydrogen storage. (7) Steam driven electric power generation is old, well known, safe and reliable for centuries to come. Solar Thermal Power is the safest option of any other conventional form of energy production such as nuclear, coal or natural gas. (8) Solar thermal can not only generate electricity but also could be used to extract hydrogen from water. (9) It is cost competitive with traditional energy plants, and is by far the most economical and reliable choice when the cost of warming the atmosphere is included in the calculations. With climate change costing billions of dollars in destruction each year, we need to use true cost accounting in energy production.

One of the World's Largest Solar Thermal Power Plants

On October 26, 2010, *The Los Angeles Times* reported that the Obama Administration announced approval of a 1,000 Megawatt solar power plant on federal land in southern

California. This will be one of the world's largest solar plants at a cost of $6 billion dollars. Instead of being built by an American firm, it will be developed by Solar Millennium, a German firm, with co-developer Chevron Energy Solutions. This solar project shows that there are going to be very large projects with good paying jobs. This project will create 1,000 jobs for construction and 300 permanent jobs, plus many more by suppliers. This project will supply electricity to 300,000 houses.

Scaling Up Solar Power on a Grand Scale: Desertec

A grand vision by the Desertec Foundation is to impound the abundance of sunlight in North Africa to supply 15% of Europe's energy by 2050. To transfer the energy, engineers have developed switches that can sustain 800 kilovolts, enabling High Voltage Direct Current (HVDC) lines to move current up to 4,000 kilometers with energy losses of only 10%-15%. This means that sunlight impounded in North Africa can be turned into electricity and transmitted across the Mediterranean Sea to Europe. An article on this project, "Sending African Sunlight to Europe, Special Delivery", was published on August 13, 2010 in *Science* magazine.

This means that solar thermal electricity can be transmitted, via HVDC from the sunlit Western United States, up to 4,000 kilometers (2,484 miles). It is 2,462 road miles from Las Vegas to Washington, D.C. It is clear that the sunlight generated in the Western states, including Utah, can transmit electricity to any point in the lower 48 States and Alaska. Hawaii can generate its electric power from its own abundant sunlight, wind power and hydrogen from the surrounding ocean. The use of centralized electric power generation by worker-owner corporations can be seen as a contributing part of the larger Third Industrial Revolution, defined above, by Jeremy Rifkin.

Tunisia to Transmit Solar Power Electricity to Italy

With the endorsement of the Desertec Foundation, NUR Energie has launched the TuNur project using solar thermal energy to link Tunisia to Italy via an HDCV cable that will supply a constant 2,000 MW of electricity. When completed, TuNur is set to be the world's largest solar energy project. The announcement was posted on huffingtonpost.com in an article by Vivian Norris, "Here Comes the Sun: Tunisia to Energize Europe" on 1/28/2012.[20]

As quoted in Ms. Norris's article, the director of Desertec Foundation, Dr. Thiemo Gropp added: "TuNur will benefit Tunisa by creating jobs and spurring investments in local education to aid the long term management of the plants after 2016. With this important first step, we are showing the world's governments, industries and consumers that what many thought to be science fiction is actually science fact. We hope that this is the first of many more such plants to be built in the desert regions of the world."

Desertec's engineers have used several studies about the generation of electric power and have concluded that the best choice is "concentrating solar power", or solar thermal. "Concentrating Solar Power looks from every side to be a very effective method", according to Hani El Nokraschy, a German-based business man who has been involved in the Desertec project since the late 1990s. Bernard Milow, with the German Aerospace Center has said that solar thermal power plants located in prime locations can produce electricity at 9-11 cents per KWH. The U.S. average price was 12 cents in 2013, for residential electricity, according to a state-by-state analysis by the Public Policy Institute of New York State, Inc.

Generation IV Nuclear Reactors May Dispose of Nuclear Waste

Generation IV nuclear reactors are being designed technologically to solve all of the problems formerly long associated with nuclear power—safety, cost, efficiency, waste, uranium scarcity and even the threat of terrorism. Most importantly, these new fast breeder reactors can provide power for the next one thousand years by burning and disposing of depleted uranium and spent fuel rods in the world's huge stockpiles.

As reported in the book, *Abundance*, "With coinvestments from Bill Gates and venture capitalist Vinod Khosla, Nathan Myhrvold founded TerraPower to develop the Traveling Wave

Reactor (TWR), a generation IV variation that he calls 'the world's most simplified passive fast breeder reactor.' The TWR has no moving parts, can't melt down, and can run safely for fifty-plus years, literally without human intervention. It can do all this while requiring no more enrichment operations, zero spent fuel handling, and no reprocessing or waste storage facilities. What's more the reactor vessel can serve as the unit's (robust) burial casket. Essentially, TWRs are a "build, bury and forget" power supply for a region or city, making them ideal for the developing world.[21]

Myhrvold recognizes the size of this challenge, but he correctly points out that "'If we're going to reach our goal of energy abundance, places like Africa and India are where the massive increase will be needed the most. This is exactly why we've designed these reactors with safe, easy-to-maintain, and proliferation-proof features. We have to make them appropriate for use in the developing world." He also cites the enormous benefit of disposing of existing nuclear waste, which has plagued the world with no solution in sight for so long.

The goal is to have a demonstration unit up and running by 2020. Most importantly, Myhrvold thinks that the power provided by TWRs can be priced lower than coal, which is exactly what investors need to spread them around the world, while dramatically decreasing global warming. Between now and 2020, the world will need to leave fossil fuels in the ground and build solar and wind power at a scale that will hold global warming in check until Traveling Wave Reactors can begin to serve the developing nations as well.

Full Cost Pricing

Lester Brown, president of the Earth Policy Institute wrote: "The key to restructuring the economy is to get the market to tell the truth through full-cost pricing. If the world is to move onto a sustainable path, we need economists who will calculate indirect cost and work with political leaders to incorporate them into market prices by restructuring taxes. For energy specifically, full-cost pricing means putting a tax on carbon to reflect the full cost of burning fossil fuels. Some 2,500 economists, including nine Nobel Prize winners in economics, have endorsed the concept of tax shifts.

When added together, the many indirect costs to society – including climate change, oil industry tax breaks, military protection of oil supply, oil industry subsidies, oil spills and treatment of auto exhaust-related respiratory illnesses—total roughly 12 dollars per gallon. That is on top of the price paid at the pump. These are real costs. Someone bears them. If not us, our children."[22]

Photovoltaic Electricity Is Now Cheaper than a Diesel Generator

Recent figures from market analysts with Bloomberg New Energy Finance, show that the price of solar panels fell by almost 50 per cent in 2011, resulting from economies of scale. That makes them a cost-effective option for people in developing countries. In India, electricity from solar, supplied to the grid, is now cheaper than from diesel generators.

Natural Gas, as a Transitional Fuel, Has CO2 Emissions that Are Too High

Natural gas is being touted as emitting 50% less CO2 than coal and proponents claim that we should buy time to reduce CO2 emissions by using natural gas as a transition energy source. This argument sounds good until you look at the numbers and the alternatives. David Strahan, in his article, *"The Great Gas Showdown"*[23], shows that the reduction in CO2 from natural gas is highly over-rated:

"According to the US Argonne National Laboratory, over its life cycle—from source to use—petrol emits 334 grams of CO2, (gCO2eq) for every kilowatt of energy it contains, compared with Compressed Natural Gas's 297 grams." *This reveals that natural gas is only an 11% improvement over oil in terms of CO2 emissions.* It is **not** "clean energy" as it is constantly advertised on TV.

"In all-electric mode, the Volt is responsible for emissions of 168 gCO2eq/km, which is fractionally lower than a CNG-powered Civic. The all-electric Nissan Leaf does still better, accounting for just 160 gCO2eq/km. So even now gas cannot match electricity for cutting emissions from cars. What's more, if the Leaf is charged up in Europe—where grid power emits less carbon than in the US—the Leaf's emissions fall to 99gCO2eq/km. And emissions from electric cars will keep falling as power generation gets cleaner. Compressed natural gas, however, is a dead end for reducing emissions. Clearly, the case for natural gas as a bridging fuel to a low-carbon future is far weaker than the industry would have us believe."[24]

David Strahan also shows that the US electricity grid produces 755 power plant CO2 emissions when compared to the 467 power plant emissions in the European electricity grid. Obviously, we need to replace the dirty US electricity grid with cleaner renewable power sources to drive our cars and service our homes and businesses.

THE ONLY WAY TO STOP SEA LEVEL RISE IS TO STOP BURNING FOSSIL FUELS BY SHIFTING TO RENEWABLE ENERGY POWER

Sea Level Rise of Four Feet Is Locked In—Inevitable

We may be closer to extinction than you may know or realize, because climate change increases global temperature gradually, but it locks in catastrophic destruction long into the future. For example, an international team of scientists led by Anders Levermann, published a study that found that for every one degree Fahrenheit of global warming due to carbon pollution, global average sea level will rise by more than 4 feet in the long run.

We have two sea levels: the sea level of today, and the sea level that is already being locked in for some distant tomorrow.

Levermann, and his colleagues at Climate Central, published this report in the *Proceedings of the National Academy of Sciences* on September 2, 2013. It concludes as follows:

"To begin with, it appears that the amount of carbon pollution to date has already locked in more than 4 feet of sea level rise past today's levels. That is enough, at high tide, to submerge more than half of today's population in 316 coastal cities and towns (home to 3.6 million) in the lower 48 states."

"By the end of this century, if global warming emissions continue to increase, that may lock in 23 feet of sea level rise, and threaten 1,429 municipalities that would be mostly submerged at high tide. Those cities have a total population of 18 million."[25]

This report concludes that within a rapidly closing window, rapid and deep cuts in carbon emissions may avoid some of these consequences. The global temperature rise to date is 1.53 degrees Fahrenheit. The cost of not taking immediate action soars into trillions of dollars from coastal property destruction, globally. The cost of caring for the refugees and helping them to rebuild their lives is not included.

The Oceans Are Acidifying at an unparalleled Rate

Scientists have warned of the risk to marine life and our food supply as climate change causes the oceans to acidify at the fastest rate in 300 million years. Oceans currently absorb a quarter of all CO_2 emissions, and at these levels of the gas in the atmosphere increase, so does the rate at which it dissolves in seawater, making the water more acidic. This is known as global warming's "evil twin."

"The potentially disastrous consequences for the food chain have been highlighted by Professor Jean-Pierre Gattuso of the National Centre for Scientific Research in France. Their forecasts suggest that by 2018, 10 percent of the ocean will be corrosively acidic, rising to 50 percent in 2050. By 2100 the entire Arctic Ocean will be inhospitable to shellfish, they predict, as it would disrupt the ability of shellfish to grow their shells."[26]

At this rate, in your grandchildren's lifetime, we may have to take scallops, oysters, shrimp, and mussels off of the restaurant menus—and all ocean life dies--to our ultimate shame. "This is extremely worrying", Professor Gattuso told the Oceans of Tomorrow Conference in Barcelona.

The Curious Case of "Not Knowing"

A recent poll revealed that 4 out of 5 Americans now understand that global warming is caused by burning fossil fuels. Why do some members of Congress and certain corporations not see these facts about oil depletion and manmade global warming? Frank Sheed, in his book, *Theology and Sanity*,[27] so insightfully pointed out that there are three defects of the intellect:

> (1) Not knowing, (2) knowing but not realizing, (3) realizing but not adverting to what is realized. That is to say, not taking action on what is known and realized.

It is a "miracle of not knowing" by those *who choose to not know* the proven facts of concerned scientists, who continually publish papers and speak out to politicians around the globe. The temperature of the entire globe has gone up each of the last 34 years and the Earth's average temperature will rise to 3.2 to 7.2 degrees Fahrenheit by the end of 2100, depending in part on how much CO_2 we emit between now and then. This forecast was provided by Intergovernmental Panel on Climate Change (IPCC). This panel is made up of hundreds of scientists from around the world and it has tracked the growing mountain of evidence in a way that no individual scientist possibly could.

But the answer is equally clear about why there is this "miracle of not knowing" by politicians and some unenlightened businessmen: they simply love money and the ease with which they acquire it at the unheeded expense of our children and the nation. One has to ask: "Could there be ego and enormous self-indulgence involved in this curious case of not knowing?" With fossil fuel corporations pouring millions of dollars per year on Members of Congress, they also have "money blinders" on their eyes and minds.

The Global Race to Save Our Only Home Is Underway

The question arises, "Is there something or someone more powerful than the money men with their "money blinders"? Well, Mother Nature and God have certainly been closing in for some time, and this may offer some insight. Men do not control the universe and they must learn not to burn fossil fuels or we march to extinction. God controls the universe and God has made us to be evolving co-creators with compassion and empathy.

We are witnessing one natural disaster after another, around the globe, requiring people from other countries to help the walking wounded, the suffering, the survivors and thousands of refugees, who are suddenly without resources or a livelihood. Compassion, empathy and justice are being drawn out of us around the globe to assist people caught in one devastation event after another. Christ's last commandment to "Love one another as I have loved you," is being drawn out of men and women of good will at an accelerating pace.

The money men, and women, love their money, so they cannot see that their money has enslaved them. This is indeed an obvious addiction by some of our so-called corporate and political "leaders." If the ideals of peace, compassion and justice do not have any weight on their balance scale, perhaps their own survival and the survival of the nations will. So be it. They will not prevail over time. But we need to break their control over what is important to us and our children now. We must prevail, or the addicted-to-money-and-power men and women will take us down with them and the entire species of humans will be extinct. As "Bucky" Fuller warned us in 1969, we must stop being lethally ignorant about our good energy resources and use sun power globally before we become "cosmically bankrupt."

The world's scientists, physicists, biologists, chemists and engineers have moved rapidly to achieve the global shift to wind, biofuels and Sun power. Now is the time to dedicate a sufficient amount of taxpayer's dollars to the task of advancing the forward days of all humans, though producing renewable energy. Of course, the mind-boggling short-sightedness of some of our Members of Congress must be transformed into having intelligent long range planning fever. Our Congressional representatives need to develop a fever for advancing the forward days of the people that they have been elected to represent, or they must be replaced by Representatives and Senators who care and declare that they will advance bills in Congress that will shift taxpayer dollars to renewable energy.

A steady flow of cheap oil has been the major source of the rise of American wealth, through the 1950's and up to the

1980's. American families enjoyed that climb and then saw their wages stagnate for the next 30 years. Cheap oil has been a *priceless limited grub stake* for the development of humanity. A 42 gallon barrel of petroleum does work equivalent to two manual laborers employed for a whole year, according to Alan Matthews.

"Two such workers developed some 400 horse power hours yielding 1,000,000 BTU's of energy. That is the effective energy in a barrel of oil, after four-fifths is deducted for transportation, processing and heat loss." [28] The use of cheap oil, for decades, replaced so much labor, in terms of man and woman hours that Americans were enjoying increasing wealth. Those days are over for cheap oil. Our safety factor is rapidly vanishing in the next three decades. All world leaders of all nations should know how crucial that limited steady flow of oil is to the well-being of their nations.

Let the Wind and Sun Do the Work

One horse power equals 735.7 watts, according to Wikipedia. Expensive oil power can and will be replaced by renewable energy. Then, the nations can all grow together with an inexpensive energy source driving their economic systems and raising the standard of living world-wide. One can even envision a world without war, when every nation has energy from the wind and Sun to do much of the work, while providing sustainable livelihoods.

The United States Is Competitive in Manufacturing for Global Trade

The Bureau of Labor Statistics (BLS) has published a report that reveals that the United States can be competitive in global trade with many nations.

The hourly compensation costs, in manufacturing, in U.S. dollars for 2010 was as follows:

Norway	57.53
Denmark	45.48
Sweden	43.81
Germany	43.76
France	40.55
Canada	35.67
U.S	34.74
Korea	16.62
Taiwan	8.36
Mexico	6.23

Note: China was omitted from this report and was reported separately, due to difficulties with factors of comparison by the BLS.[29]

As cited above, the General Motors Union and the United Steel Workers have begun collaboration with Mondragon. In Part 4, we will examine the necessity of shifting large amounts of funding from the military to nation building at home.

PART 4

SHIFTING MONEY FROM THE MILITARY TO NATION BUILDING AT HOME

The Nation Builder's Industrial Complex

The stage is set then, for the federal government and the private sector to lead the nation to build wind farms, solar/hydrogen fuel cell kits for homes and offices, solar thermal power plants, hydrogen/electric cars and rapid transit systems. This will require a new smart electrical grid to enable everyone to plug-in. There is now a demand path for many of the Military Industrial Complex (MIC) corporations to make the long, but rapid shift, to develop the "Nation Builder's Industrial Complex".

Certainly, there will still be a need for defending the nation from terrorist attacks and cyberattacks. However, the vast majority of military spending has been based on existing and future *land wars on foreign soil against sovereign nations.* The U.S. has 268 military installations in Germany, and, approximately a total of over 950 bases spread around the world. Approximately 450,000 U.S. servicemen and women are currently deployed in more than 150 countries. The U.S. cannot be invaded on land except through Canada and Mexico. The U.S. is protected by the Pacific and the Atlantic from the east and the west, which is strongly guarded by the Air Force, the

Navy and the Coast Guard. We have a strong military defense, undeniably. Abraham Lincoln said:

"America will never be destroyed from the outside. If we falter and lose our freedoms it will be because we destroyed ourselves."

The Cold War has been long over. The vast majority of these military bases are largely based on the premise that the "projection of military power" has served the advancement of *international corporations of America* and the outsourcing of American manufacturing. This has proven to be a great mistake in terms of the need for nation building at home, which is, today, the real national defense of American families, and individuals who pay the taxes that support a monumentally wasteful and counterproductive Military Industrial Complex. The military has literally run out of enemy targets that it can easily attack and derive a substantial gain above its losses, especially in terms of American public and world opinion.

Defense Secretary Gates Blasted the Wars in Iraq and Afghanistan

The former Secretary of Defense, Robert Gates, bluntly told an audience of West Point cadets: "Any future defense secretary who advises the president to again send a big American land army into Asia or into the Middle East or Africa should have his head examined."[1]

Robert Gates has blasted wars like Iraq and Afghanistan as serious mistakes, in what was his farewell speech before retiring, Gates has set the stage for a major withdrawal of American forces from these two unsustainable wars, which President Obama has implemented. This can lead to a substantial decrease in military spending, as the troops come home and many of the estimated 950 military bases around the world can now be closed. The stage is set to transfer Pentagon dollars to alternative energy and infrastructure building at home. As we close bases and bring the troops home we can provide good paying jobs for them in the Nation Builder's Industrial Complex.

The global economic crisis has demonstrated that an economy based solely on artificial financial wealth, moved around in financial markets, rather than investment in home-grown manufacturing and livelihoods at home, does not work. It is important that American international corporations return home and be based in America, making things and, thereby, creating sustainable livelihood systems at home.

The Government Must Shift Resources from Warring to the Domestic Economy

The taxpayers in the U.S. cannot afford to maintain military forces at the same level, or even close to the same level for four major reasons: (1) Global investments, by American corporations and unwitting American workers are dramatically driving up the price of oil for Americans and the military; (2) We are becoming a bankrupt country, largely due to the seemingly endless war in Afghanistan, and plans for more wars driven by the entrenched profiteering of the Military Industrial Complex (MIC); (3) The rapidly increasing costs of oil will not only affect the military, as American civil society will face the same, very expensive transition from oil to renewable energies; (4) Social Security and Medicare are very popular earned benefits and totally necessary for Americans to have a minimum of personal financial security and basic health service and they certainly will not be cut deeply enough to reduce the $14 trillion national deficit *while maintaining an enormous "national security" budget;* (5) The transition from petroleum to renewable energy, over the next three decades will require a total national commitment, both public and private, of trillions of dollars; (6) The top priority of the nation now is to save the nation from economic collapse. It is now starkly clear that millions of Americans must shift out of the MIC and have new non-military jobs to build a totally new energy and transportation system, using alternative energy, to get to their jobs. America's real "national interests" in defending the nation, are the shift from unproductive military ventures and the destructive arms trade to providing alternative energy and good sustainable jobs at home.

The Real National Security Budget Is
$1.2 Trillion per Year

America is nearly bankrupt largely because of runaway "national security" spending and the banking disasters of 2008. The real national security budget is far more than the $700 billion for the Pentagon budget and the war-fighting supplementary funds for our conflicts in Iraq and Afghanistan. According to a detailed accounting by Christopher Hellman with the Center for Arms Control and Non-Proliferation, the total National Security Budget is $1.2 trillion a year.[2]

Here is the breakdown listed by Hellman: this accounting includes $700 billion for the Pentagon, $40 billion for the intelligence agencies; $71.6 billion for "Homeland Security"; $129 billion for veterans programs to care for them after they return from the wars; $18 billion for foreign affairs and counterterrorist budgets; $48.5 billion for military and Defense Department retirees and $185 billion in *interest payments* on borrowing related to *past Pentagon spending*. All of this totals over $1.2 trillion per year. Throwing money at the military is clearly an unsustainable expenditure and many members of Congress are just starting to embrace that fact.

Shifting Destructive Arms Production to Constructive
Energy Projects

The production of arms, military jets, gunships, tanks, guns, etc. is a global sales industry, with the U.S. providing an estimated 40% to 78% (depending on the year) of the global production of lethal weaponry which can *only* be used for the destruction of people, military facilities and equipment, infrastructure, buildings and productive resources, all around the world. The U.S. sold $85.3 billion in arms sales in 2011 according to the non-partisan Congressional Research Service. Most sales went to the Gulf region, the most unstable, violent part of the world. This only fuels deadly violence.

Strategically, the Military Industrial Complex (MIC) has placed production plants and warehouses in every state, so that the Members of Congress, in each state, will vote to maintain the jobs that are producing these destructive arms. However, now the military knows that many of these aircraft and vehicles cannot even be used! They will simply not have enough affordable petroleum supplies. Future large scale land wars are wisely opposed by the former Secretary of Defense and many of these aircraft and vehicles were designed to serve large scale land wars—boots on the ground.

The Pentagon has told Congress that they no longer need or want the C-17, and the F-35 jet fighters, however, enough Members of Congress have voted to keep these unwanted weapons of destruction in production, in order to keep jobs in their states. This is how billions of our taxpayer dollars are wasted each year. Those days should be clearly over.

Constructive Work for the MIC Is Now a National Emergency Priority

Congress obviously needs to provide the MIC employees and returning troops with more constructive employment that actually serves the nation. The problem has been that the production of weapons results in such a large profit and such large salaries that it is difficult to shift weapons production to peacetime jobs and profits. In order to make this shift, it will be necessary to undertake projects on a large scale that will benefit the nation and provide employment for the former MIC employees with good but not huge salaries. As it turns out, our national emergency needs for a totally new energy system, new electric grid, transportation system and infrastructure largely fit these requirements.

Military Spending is the Weakest Job Creator

An independent analysis by Robert Polin and Heidi Garret-Peltier at the University of Massachusetts concluded that military spending was the weakest job creator compared with creating jobs on clean energy, health care, education or simply returning the money to the private economy in the form of tax cuts.[3]

The Transformation of Consciousness about War

At the close of the 20th century, Richard J. Barnet wrote a powerful article titled, "REFLECTIONS after the Cold War", which was published by the *New Yorker.*[4] Barnet was the founder of the Institute for Policy Studies. Barnet transitioned to the afterlife in 2009. What follows are excerpts from that article, which are relevant today. Barnet wrote:

"Since the early years of the century, a long process of rethinking has been underway about the uses of military power to advance national political and economic interests. Gorbachev's "new thinking" is grounded in some of the obvious lessons of the twentieth century. The First World War nearly obliterated the distinction between victors and vanquished; Britain and France suffered such grievous casualties and economic costs that they could sustain neither their empires nor stable economies and robust democracies at home. The Second World War made it clear that high-technology "conventional warfare," however noble the cause, could not be repeated without reducing whole continents to rubble. It was immediately apparent that the atomic bomb was not a weapon in the strict sense, because it could be effectively used by *not* using it. Today, there is a growing consensus that a large scale nuclear war would destroy all that was to be defended."

For example, the fear-mongering about Iran obtaining nuclear missile weapons is unrealistic. The Iranians would soon discover that the use of those weapons would logically lead to the immediate destruction of their own nation and a large scale nuclear war would mean that a radiation cloud, drifting around the world would destroy much of human life. While Iran may or may not produce a nuclear weapon, it will be impossible to use it without guaranteeing its own destruction and this is true for all nations.

The anger and disillusionment of Soviet citizens over the Afghanistan invasion was a significant factor in Gorbachev's decision to end it. As we have seen, the attacks of 9/11 gave George W. Bush the public support he needed to invade Afghanistan and Iraq, which will have cost $8 trillion and will have led to a national $14 trillion deficit and the Great Recession. Barnet stated the case well: "...the United States has systematically sacrificed economic strength to the accumulation of military power. In the process the sinews of nationhood have become frayed. Neither the neglected education system of the United States nor the country's weakened industrial base can support the global role to which our national-security elites have aspired.

Running nations by a dictatorship, whether of left or right, offers no way out of poverty, but the yearning for a decent society in which people can build communities without gross exploitation, without worshipping money and defiling nature, and without creating walls between a few rich and many poor is as powerful a human impulse as it ever was." [4]

The New Focus Is to Advance Humankind's Forward Days—Not Warring

The Members of Congress should be happy to support such a paradigm shift, because they will be supporting constructive job creation by funding Solar Power Plants, hydrogen electric power storage, wind and biofuel production. This will create millions of new jobs in manufacturing, housing and housing related industries, new towns, hydrogen/electric car production and the rapid transit retrofitting of the thousands of suburbs to save them from the bulldozers. Otherwise, people cannot afford to pay the ever-rising cost of gasoline to drive to work, day care, school and shopping. The nation has already reached the economic barriers where the ownership of one car, instead of two or three per family, will advance that family's forward days. As we will see, fast surface rapid transit will be the choice of most job commuters in the future, when and where that choice is made available.

Fuels for Civilian Airlines, and Military Aircraft

If it is possible, biofuels must be rapidly scaled up to meet the enormous demand for jet fuel by a much smaller military jet force and the 357,000 aircraft in the civilian airlines industry, according to a Federal Aviation Administration estimate. It is estimated that there are about 30,000 commercial air carrier flights per day in the United States, plus 2,200 for Fed Ex and UPS. Private planes add another 27,000 flights per day. The need to scale up the quantity of biofuels for aircraft is now glaringly obvious, and very difficult.

The U.S. Naval Research Laboratory has developed a technology for simultaneously extracting carbon dioxide and hydrogen from sea water and converting the two gases to a liquid hydrocarbon fuel as a replacement for jet fuel. The predicted cost is $3 to $6 per gallon and could be commercially viable within seven to ten years.[5]

The main hope rests with the incredible history of inventions, using our metaphysical intellects, to create new ways In order to meet the challenge. History also tells us that the greatest advance in the innovations in the U.S. came from investing in education through the G.I. Bill.

A New "G.I. Bill" for Education

It will take a huge transfer of physicists, biologists, engineers, planners and management personnel from the MIC to the Nation Builder's Industrial Complex to begin to meet this long term, on-going demand for biofuel, or other technology, to fly our nation's aircraft, as well as all of the other pressing domestic needs that have been too long neglected. The nation will need the equivalent of a G.I. Bill to provide education for those who will meet our new energy demands in pure science and applied science, engineers and especially, long range planners. The Nation Builders Industrial Complex will need urban regional planners, and livelihood systems economists to develop the regional economies and infrastructures that will guide the shift from the MIC to productive projects at home and a whole new sustainable worker/owner cooperative system.

Rebuilding the American Transportation System

In 2008, it was estimated that there were about 137 million registered automobiles in the United States, and 110 million trucks, totaling 247 million vehicles. They need to be replaced with hydrogen/electric powered vehicles. There are approximately 16 million new cars sold in the U.S. each year and in good times about 3 million trucks for a total of 19 million vehicles. At that rate of production, it will take 13 to 15 years to replace those vehicles with hydrogen/ electric power, such as the Daimler fuel cell technology and/or the Testa Electric car. This is not counting the 4 million, or more, buses for Bus Rapid Transit systems, and mini-buses that will be in high demand for suburbanites to get to work, school and shopping.

This raises the question, "How many years does the U.S. have before gasoline prices become unaffordable for the driving public to get to their necessary destinations?" It becomes quickly obvious that we must undertake this enormous task immediately in order to outrace the energy crisis over the next 15-30 years after reaching Peak Oil in 2006. That would require the Administration, Congress, the Supreme Court and the American public to know, realize and decide to take decisive action to meet this national emergency. The funds can only be found by raising taxes on the super-rich and by shifting large amounts of the military budget to the Nation Builder's Industrial Complex. For those who say, "Good luck with that," it should be clear that getting to your job and the total economic collapse of the nation is at stake. This is not a difficult political decision. Shifting from fossil fuels to renewable energy is a necessary political decision. Delay is not an option.

Meteorologists Announce that Human Activity Is Causing Climate Change

The American Meteorological Society (your local weather men and weather women) has updated their official stance on the relationship between climate change and weather events. "Observations show increases in globally averaged air and ocean temperatures, as well as widespread melting of snow and ice and rising globally averaged sea level." These changes "are beyond what can be explained by the natural variability of climate."

They continue: "It is clear from extensive scientific evidence that the dominant cause of the rapid change in climate of the past half century is human-induced increases in the amount of atmospheric greenhouse gases, including carbon dioxide (CO_2), chlorofluorocarbons, methane and nitrous oxide. The most important of these over the long term is CO_2, whose concentration in the atmosphere is rising principally as a result of fossil-fuel combustion and deforestration."[6]

We cannot keep sending 90 billion tons of carbon dioxide into the greenhouse roof, while adding billions of tons each year, simply because it increases the warming and leads to a life that you do not want for yourself, your children, grandchildren and their offspring to have to survive under those extreme and terrifying conditions.

Well, perhaps I am over estimating the blindness of the rich, even for the benefit of their own offspring. I certainly hope that is not the case. If the rich and the 600 oil industry lobbyists cannot overcome their blindness, well, we, the public, will just have to do it for them, and we will. In fact, the Millenials (those born between 1982 and 2003), their children and grandchildren will predictably bring that change about because it is their future that will be so radically affected. The action of our youth is a delightful, life-giving action. I hope that it will be celebrated in every pub and joyful place in the world.

The Big Picture

An article by James Fallows, "DIRTY COAL, CLEAN FUTURE", was published in the December 2010 edition of *The Atlantic*.[7] Fallows describes the rate of rise in CO2 as follows:

"Before James Watt invented the steam engine in the late 1700s—the concentration of carbon dioxide in the atmosphere was around 280 parts per million (meaning 280 carbon-dioxide molecules per million molecules of "dried air", or air with the water removed.) By 1900, as Europe and America were industrializing, it had reached about 300 parts per million.

Now the carbon-dioxide concentration is at or above 400 ppm, which is the highest level in many millions of years. We know that the last time CO2 was sustained at this level, much of the Greenland and West Antarctic ice sheets were not there, Michael Mann, a climate scientist at Penn State, reported.

450 Parts per Million is the Safety Limit According to the Intergovernmental Panel on Climate Change (IPCC)

The IPCC, the body of the world's leading climate scientists convened by the United Nations, reported that if the full range of renewable technologies were deployed, the world could keep greenhouse gas concentrations to less than 450 parts per million, the level that scientists have predicted will be the limit of safety beyond which climate change becomes catastrophic and irreversible.

"The main uncertainties involve what might happen as carbon-dioxide levels reach 450 ppm and above. In particular, the question is how and when "positive feedback" loops would kick in, so that the hotter things get, the faster they will get even hotter." The main way this would happen would be through the melting of the polar ice sheets, which would mean less white ice surface to reflect the sun's heat, and more blue water to absorb it."[8]

The Permafrost Melt Will Be Irreversible Without Major Fossil Fuel Cuts in the Immediate Future

All of that additional heat threatens to light the fuse of the world's biggest "carbon bomb", the vast permafrost region spanning 9 million square kilometers across Alaska, Canada, Siberia and parts of northern Europe.

With the melting of the permafrost in the far northlands, which releases huge quantities of methane gas, scientists can already see the probability of setting up a positive feedback loop, where methane joins CO2 to build up the greenhouse effect, increasing global temperature rapidly, which in turn, melts more vast areas of permafrost, and so on.

The Massive Release of Methane in the Arctic Has Already Begun

"Dramatic and unprecedented plumes of methane—a greenhouse gas 20 times more potent than carbon dioxide— have been seen bubbling to the surface of the Arctic Ocean by scientists undertaking an extensive survey of the region. The scale and volume of the methane release has astonished the head of the Russian research team who has been surveying the seabed of the East Siberian Arctic Shelf off Russia for nearly 20 years." This was reported on December 14, 2011, in an exclusive interview by *The Independent/UK,* with Igor Semiletov, of the Eastern branch of the Russian Academy of Sciences, who reported to The Independent (UK) "that he has never before witnessed the scale and force of the methane being released from beneath the Arctic seabed.

"This is the first time that we found continuous, powerful and impressive seeping structures, more than 1,000 meters in diameter. In a very small area, less than 10,000 square miles, we have counted more than 100 fountains, or torch-like structures, bubbling through the water column and injected directly into the atmosphere from the seabed," Dr. Semiletov said.[9]

With this scientific observation of the massive release of methane in the Arctic, the siren for emergency action is now blasting away. Climate deniers and fossil fuel lobbyists take note, because from this day forward we must replace fossil fuels as quickly as possible to avoid more severe harm to the people on Planet Earth. The planet has indeed reached and passed the "for Christ's sake line." The equivalent of the canary in the coal mine has already died.

The Time for Political and Economic Action Is Upon Us

The International Panel on Climate Change (IPCC) Landmark Study published on May 9, 2011, projected that renewable energy could account for almost 80% of the world's energy supply within four decades, but only if governments pursue the policies needed to promote renewable energy.[10] The investment that will be needed to avoid more devastation is likely to amount to $5 trillion globally in the next decade and $7 trillion from 2021 to 2030. However, this is entirely doable because the investment will represent only 1 percent of global Gross Domestic Product (GDP). Renewable energy will play a greater role than either nuclear or carbon capture and storage by 2050, the scientists predict. We have already reached 400 ppm and the permafrost melt down will set up an irreversible feedback loop if we do start leaving fossil fuels in the ground, immediately.

The synopsis of the Intergovernmental Panel on Climate Change report that would be presented to governments had to be agreed upon line by line and word by word unanimously by all countries. This was done at the May 9, 2011 meeting in Abu Dhabi. No government or scientist represented can say that they disagree with the finished findings, which is the strength of this United Nations' report.

The top international priority is to stop raising the global temperature before we reach another "tipping point", after which there is no possible return to normal life on Earth on a human life scale. It is not too late to stop the temperature rise. However, now we will have to live through more of the devastating impacts that are already in the pipeline, such as Katrina, Super storm Sandy and extremely harsh winters.

When science showed us these facts it became clear that the human cost of burning coal, oil and natural gas has become so high as to threaten all life on the planet. There will be no people left on this Earth to sell or buy coal and oil if we were so insane as to continue down this path. Insanity has a very high cost, so let's include it in our cost/benefit analysis of what is economical, as if *price* was the issue! The issue is survival and advancing our human days and hopefully, a happier life of *shared economic and spiritual wealth on the planet.*

Solar Thermal Power and Wind Can Replace Coal-Fired Power Plants

There are approximately 300 coal-fired electric plants in the United States. Replacing them with 100% solar thermal/wind power is one of the fastest tracks, known to date, to rapidly reduce the ominous threat to billions of people by raising the global temperature to the tipping point. Solar power and wind turbines can also be coupled with hydrogen storage to directly eliminate fossil fuel consumption when the sun is not shining, and the wind is not blowing to maintain peak power capability. this is the lowest cost option and the most sustainable option for investors in energy production when full cost accounting is applied.

National Mobilization: A New Culture for Americans

Advancing a National Long Range Energy and Transportation Plan in the U.S. is largely the job of the President, a functioning Congress, educators, religious leaders and the national mainstream media. Otherwise, it will be difficult to educate and mobilize the entire country to meet the fast-closing energy crunch and to shift military spending to the task of Nation Building at Home, beginning in the next few years.

President Obama Announces that "Oil Is the Fuel of the Past"

On March 7, 2012, President Obama began to promote his new energy policy in a speech in Mount Holly, N.C. The

President called on Congress to give $1 billion for energy efficient technologies.[11]

The administration's goal is to make electric vehicles as affordable and convenient as gasoline powered vehicles by 2020. President Obama made his most urgent appeal yet for the nation to wean itself from oil, calling it a "fuel of the past".[11] The gasoline price crunch at $3.92 per gallon in April 2012 was already worrying the public as expert's predictions of gas prices rising to $5.00 during the Summer months was not what the public wanted to hear.

There are a large number of well-informed people waiting for more transparency and truth-telling-to-power to happen in the mainstream media. This essential change, in what we are told by the mainstream media, has just begun to happen, as of this writing in May, 2014. Some mention of climate change is becoming more common.

However, NOVA, a Public Broadcasting System program, has presented a very good picture of the scientific realization that if and when the western part of Antarctica melts we will never recover life on the tiny Planet Earth as we know it. They have taken deep drilled core samples and the analysis of these scientists shows that the temperatures of the past show vividly that if the western part of Antarctica melts, and parts of the eastern part melt, the seas will rise by an estimated 23 feet. On May 13, 2014, scientific experts announced that "the collapse of large parts of the ice sheet in West Antarctic has begun and is almost certainly unstoppable with global warming accelerating the pace of the melting."[12]

This projection into the future does not alarm people nearly as much as gasoline prices rising to $5.00 per gallon, or more, which also leads to rising food costs around the globe. As Jeremy Rifkin pointed out, at $147 per barrel national economies shut down because people and businesses cannot afford the price and they stop buying. As a result, the entire economic system shuts down, takes a break and waits for gas prices to fall. Gas prices then fall, food prices fall and whole economic systems around the world begin to grow until they reach that oil price of $147 per barrel and then, global economic systems collapse once again. Then the cycle begins again. Only the shift to renewable energies can save us from this decline of the oil driven economic systems around the world.

The mobilization of the nations will require great reflection and truthful reporting by the mainstream media, the governments around the world, the world-wide corporate leaders, the major financial institutions, major investors, OPEC, China, India, Brazil, Asia, South America, the Pope and the leaders of Islam. It will also require fast moving CHANGE! Delay in implementation of a Global Energy and Transportation Plan is the greatest threat to American citizens and the entire global economy. The pace of this change must be accelerated in order to prevent the panic situation that politicians fear the most. That would be when their constituents occupy their offices and the entire hallway, and they insist on sane, intelligent, and wise action, now.

Robert Kunzig wrote: "Methane in the atmosphere warms the Earth over 20 times more per molecule than carbon dioxide does, then after a decade or two, it oxidizes to CO2 and keeps on warming for a long time. Many scientists think just that kind of scenario might occur today: The warming caused by burning fossil fuels could trigger a runaway release of methane from the deep sea and the frozen north."[13] As we have seen, the massive release of methane in the Arctic sea has already begun.

James Zachos, University of California, Santa Cruz states: "With fossil fuels today…we're taking what took millions of years to accumulate and releasing it in a geologic instant."

The burning of coal and other fossil fuels cost trillions, in known existent and future losses globally, that are not in our existing accounting of the cost of electricity per kilowatt hour. For those who would deny global warming, it does not matter if this is happening, *in part,* by some unknown source, (such as weather cycles) because *we know that man-made sources are adding to the rise in the world's temperature and we must stop it at all costs.* Given the facts, the hearts and souls of men and women around the world, must begin to melt through comprehension and compassion, and be moved to action.

Insurance Companies Confirm the Growing Risks and Costs of Climate Change

Representatives of the nation's top insurance companies took a strong position at a Senate meeting in early March, 2012 confirming that the costs both to taxpayers and businesses, from extreme weather events will continue to climb due to the irrefutable march of global warming resulting from climate change.

Cynthia McHale, the insurance program director for Ceres, made to most clear statement: "Our climate is changing, human activity is helping to drive the change, and the cost of these extreme weather events are going to keep ballooning unless we break through our political paralysis, and bring down emissions that are warming our planet. If we continue on this path, extreme weather is certain to cause more homes and businesses to be uninsurable in the private insurance market, leaving the costs to taxpayers or individuals."[14]

IS IT ACCEPTABLE TO ALLOW OIL AND GAS COMPANIES TO DESTROY OUR PROPERTIES AND OUR LIVES?

We have already seen the billions of dollars of damage caused by global warming and the resulting climate change around the world. Insurance companies are fully aware of the increasing numbers of disasters. The American legal system, led by the Department of Justice needs to investigate this ongoing long range destruction of the oceans—and the environment—as well as the staggering cost in human lives and property. The question is: do corporations have a right to increase their wealth with no regard for the awesomely destructive results of their actions? Using the principle that their rights stop where our noses begin, I think we have a case that demands justice. With the melting of the Arctic Ocean and the discovery that the Western ice shelf of the continent of Antarctica has begun melting which locks in sea level rise and other irreversible "tipping points", we have indeed waited much too long to stop fossil fuel burning on Planet Earth. Oil, Gas and Coal companies do not have the right to destroy our sea ports and millions of ocean side properties and enforced evacuation by millions of poor people from their homes and livelihoods.

PART 5

NEW TOWN BUILDING AND SUSTAINABLE LIVELIHOODS

New Town Building and Livelihood Systems Can Create a Sustainable Economy

As we have seen, there is a serious energy crunch coming in the next three decades. Fortunately, we may have just enough time to mobilize and mount a successful response. However, we cannot solve the energy problem by simply continuing "business as usual". We will need to re-organize on a national scale and act with bold determination, to provide for each other. This national reorganization of energy production will be forced upon us due to increasing oil prices and the need to slow the rapid rise of the planet's temperature for our sake and for our children and grand-children. This can only be done through long range planning that can address multiple issues at once and provide solutions. The United States will grow in population from new births and immigration as it provides a new, more desirable and sustainable way of life for people. However, growth for the advancement of the current economic system is not the goal, as we have already seen that "business as usual" is very destructive to the environment and sustainable livelihoods.

New town planning and implementation can be an exciting new chapter in forming a whole new way of life, centered on creating sustainable livelihoods, sustainable agriculture, economic democracy in cooperatives and the development of critically needed renewable energy generation on a massive scale.

Technology, Jobs and the Future of Families

In America and around the world, there is a growing army of the unemployed and the underemployed, because technology and re-engineering of the workplace with information technology and robots are eliminating jobs at a rapid pace. Corporations have undertaken a highly destructive path of eliminating laborers by replacing them with machines and software programs. Productivity per worker has soared along with more efficiency. So far, the benefits of this endeavor have accrued to the profits of corporations and shareholders without distributing the benefits to workers. This corporate strategy has been rolled out for over 30 years without any thought or strategy to employ the millions of workers who are fired, laid off and left to seek other work for less pay. This process has been documented in detail in Jeremy Rifkin's book, *The End of Work, the Decline of the Global Labor Force and the Dawn of the Post-Market Era*, first published in 1995.[1]

It is very disturbing to see that corporations and economists have focused on increasing efficiency and productivity for greater profits with no strategy or adjustments for employing the global labor force. Shifting to renewable energy from fossil fuels will create many jobs. However, in order to create sustainable employment with decent pay for the army of the unemployed and the underemployed it will require national and regional planning and the cooperation of the nation's corporations, or their replacement with worker-owner cooperatives. We need to implement Democracy in the Workplace.

The center of this planning process may prove most productive if we aggressively plan for the development of the best kind of renewable energy for each region. For example, in the hot Southwestern region, solar thermal, solar photovoltaics and wind will work best. In the Midwest, Southeast and Northwest a combination of wind, solar thermal, and geothermal can produce enough energy to replace fossil fuels. The colder Northeast may require some energy transfers from the other regions. Detailed analysis and planning may produce different results. It may be best to follow the path of The Third Industrial Revolution chosen by the Eurozone, to distribute energy across a continental electric grid with everyone supplying energy in a collaborative, highly cooperative manner. This would enable households within neighborhood cooperatives and small businesses to produce their own energy and sell any unused portion back to the grid. Energy production and distribution in this manner would establish sustainable energy which can further support sustainable job creation in a region of cooperative businesses and families, where productivity gains are advances in pay to the worker-owners. Equality in the distribution of profits among worker-owners is long overdue.

There are hard economic "laws" concerning production. However, there are no economic "laws" that say we cannot distribute profits to workers who produce the profit on a more equitable basis. As productivity soars, based on massive amounts of renewable energy, new kinds of service jobs can be created to give livelihoods to all, so that every abled bodied person can enjoy the dignity of work.

Interlocking Problems Can Be Solved By Long Range Planning and New Towns

Instead of building onto existing cities, (with more suburbs) we can build satellite new towns that are connected to large cities by surface rapid transit systems on dedicated roadways using rubber tire rolling stock to provide maximum flexibility and affordability.

The following challenges are interlocking: (1) The need to provide livelihoods that are sustainable, just, and cooperative rather than a competitive job killing business model; (2) The need to immediately shift our national agenda to the production of renewable energy rather than waiting for our "precious grubstake" of oil and coal, natural gas and nuclear power to be overdrawn, setting the Planet Earth up for total economic collapse; (3) The need to shift our reliance on gasoline-fueled transportation to hydrogen/electric automobiles and inexpensive rapid transit systems; (4) The need to quickly curb the massive quantities of carbon dioxide and methane released into the atmosphere, causing the rise of disastrous and costly climate change; (5) The need to provide the millions of suburbanites with mini buses and a Bus Rapid Transit system so that they can get to work in the face of the on-coming, and unaffordable rise in gasoline prices (6) The need to stop suburban sprawl by building satellite new towns vertically that can combine these objectives in a new national purpose: the cooperative survival of humanity. (7) The current pattern of growth is unsustainable. We must design regional economic systems that are sustainable, and are built to provide the basic necessities of carbon free energy and transportation, clean water, top soil maintenance and nutrition, local food, shelter and employment. These are the goals and objectives of Livelihood Systems. These are also some of the main goals of the Third Industrial Revolution. It is all done by planning with Christ's values and good design.

Combining Constellations of Cooperatives with Satellite New Town Development

In order to create jobs for American workers at home, we can focus on building New Towns that eventually form Constellations of cooperative corporations. It should be noted, up front, that Mondragon style corporate charters can be signed by any business within a given region, or outside of that region.

A Constellation does *not* have to have all of its cooperating businesses located *within a given geographical region.*

For example, a Constellation affiliated cooperative can supply shrimp from the Bay Islands, off Honduras, to a Constellation in Ohio. General Motors Company (GM) or Ford can provide pick-ups to any Constellation, if they so choose, with or without a Mondragon style corporate charter. However, GM and/or Ford may see the value of building a manufacturing plant within a Constellation, with a Mondragon style corporate charter, in order to serve additional Constellations, as they are developed. Once again, access to this growing consumer base will become of interest to American entrepreneurs, perhaps even compelling, as we develop this far reaching business model and banking model that people can relate to in a way that has never been offered to them before.

A new economic synthesis can be formed between New Towns and new economic arrangements that creatively advance the wealth and sustainability of a whole region. As noted above, several Livelihood Systems New Towns can be formed so that a regional market of over one million people can produce and distribute most all of their basic necessities within that region. Working together, in cooperation, small and medium sized businesses can creatively work to produce much more for much less and distribute that new wealth in purchasing power within the Regional Constellation. The wealth produced and distributed among worker/owners in the

Constellations creates a sustainable and unique Livelihood System, substantially free of the globalized market system, in terms of supply and demand within the Constellation, as described above in Part 1.

Workers around the world, in China and Europe, the United States and the Middle East, especially, are rebelling against massive unemployment, massive firings by the tens of thousands, low wages, harsh working conditions and austerity that has been forced upon them. These brutal competition style corporations no longer serve the nations. Governments are serving the bankers who no longer serve their nations with job creating investments, but rather, gamble at the casinos that bankers, themselves, created. Derivatives and Credit Default Swaps are nothing more than ways of betting on the rise or fall of a given financial construct. They are clearly unnecessary to a nation's advancement of humankind's forward days. Therefore, they need to be outlawed as a waste of financial resources. Financial resources need to be invested in energy, transportation and sustainable employment that advance humankind's forward days.

Livelihood systems must be supplied to all. That is what the so-called "elite" and dictators are being taught around the world. Otherwise, people die from hunger. Clearly, the signs of the times, taken with a positive perspective, are that things are necessarily going to get much better, even as we back into the future.

Urban Sprawl Needs an Overhaul

When gasoline reaches $5.70 per gallon again and again, the United States will face a national crisis because we have built urban sprawl across the land, with no viable mass rapid transit systems as Europe has built. In Europe, a Euro pass can put you on a train to many destinations. Bicycles and walking are widely used because government listened to their City Planners in Europe. In the U.S. we have built our cities and roadways based on the automobile with very cheap oil, as if the price of gasoline would remain inexpensive forever. Those days are over.

Urban sprawl and the construction of highways was "social engineering with a vengeance," according to Robert Liberty, when he was executive director of 1,000 Friends of Oregon, which supports intelligent planning. Urban sprawl will be a very difficult problem to deal with, because it is so massive in scale across America. However, it is a fact that planners and engineers will have to make it as viable as possible and it will force us to have millions of hydrogen/electric cars and convenient bus rapid transit systems at affordable prices. We cannot wait until 2020 to address this massive national transportation problem. As we have seen, at $147 per barrel, the economy cannot afford the price and the flow of the entire economy shuts down.

New Towns Can Develop Inexpensive Surface Rapid Transit Systems
(And It May Be the Only Way to Save the Suburbs)

Curitiba, Brazil has developed a fast, convenient bus rapid transit system that operates like a surface Metro. It has been copied in other parts of the world. The essence of Curitiba's bus system is its speed—these buses run very frequently—some as often as 90 seconds apart, and they are reliable. The all weather stations are where you cue up to purchase your ticket. They are well-designed, attractive and the buses load and unload from a platform just like the Washington, D.C Metro, or Atlanta's Marta, except they are not underground, but rather on the surface. The vehicles are unimpeded by congested traffic or traffic signals as they operate on dedicated lanes.

About 70% of Curitiba's commuters use the Bus Rapid Transit (BRT) to travel to work. This results in streets that are not congested for those who are driving cars or riding bicycles. There are 2.2 million inhabitants of Curitiba and instead of carbon dioxide and diesel fumes choking people; the city is relatively free of air pollution. The city has designed many parks with ponds which bring nature closer to people, rather than never having contact with nature or seeing wild life. Curitiba is Brazil's 8th largest city. Curitiba's urban planning success was led by Jaime Lerner, who completed his third term as Mayor in 1992. "Imagine Rio, New York or Sao Paulo with 25 percent fewer cars," said Mr. Lerner, who studied urban planning here and in France. "We've done that here." Imagine for a moment, a city which was developed by an energetic and compassionate architect, rather than a professional politician, lawyer or ego-maniac that sought mostly their own advancement up the political ladder. That is what Jaime Lerner accomplished and his skill sets as an urban planner and mayor are legendary.

He was offered the job of Mayor by Brazil's major cities, but he declined. Curitiba's Bus Rapid Transit is designed to reach as many parts of the city as possible, and this is the key to saving the commuters in the suburbs. Minibuses routed through residential neighborhoods (read sprawling suburbs) feed passengers to conventional buses on circumferential routes, to and around the central city and on inter-district routes. Operating as the backbone of the whole system is the Bus Rapid Transit, on five main arteries, which lead to the city center, like the spokes of a wheel. To accomplish a similar design in the U.S suburbs would require giving dedicated roadways to the rapid transit system by reducing the number of roadways to cars.

Cost Considerations of the Bus Rapid Transit System

In order to design a surface rapid transit system as good as Curitiba's, one should probably learn to love and care deeply for the convenience of the rider. It is also important to go for a reasonably priced system, so that it can actually be implemented on a grand scale. Good design for rider comfort, speed, convenience and a pleasurable trip with happy people resulted in astonishing popularity of the bus over the auto in Curitiba.

According to a 1991 survey, the BRT has caused a reduction of about 27 million auto trips per year, which saved approximately 27 million liters of fuel annually. Compared to eight other cities of its size, Curitiba uses about 30 percent less fuel per capita. About 1.3 million passengers enjoy the BRT in a city of 2.2 million. Curitibanos spend about 10 percent of their income on travel, which is much below the national average.[2]

A Family Can Save $6,000 to $12,000 per Year on Transportation

With Bus Rapid Transit in the suburbs, a family could no doubt survive and thrive with one car instead of two or three. With cell phones, that one family car could be called into immediate service for any family emergency. That one car could take care of all medium and long distance travel for the family members. It would take some planning and a little sacrifice, but please take this into account: it costs an average of $6,000 per year to buy and operate a 4 year old, Honda Accord in America, at this writing. A family could save $6,000 to $12,000 per year, by using BRT and one car and have more savings to help send their blessed offspring to college.

Extensive Light Rail Transit Is Not Implemented in America for a Reason

Americans dream of having a super expensive, fixed and inflexible, light rail train come to their door and whisk them off, directly to their desired destination, which could be one of 3 to 5 destinations on that particular day. The light rail dream is simply not implementable, given the fact that the U.S. chose suburban sprawl as its downfall, based on cheap oil, which will soon be gone within the Millennial Generation's lifetimes, (those born between 1982 and 2003). They may ask, "How can people get to their workplace with the super expensive light rail dream which is impossible to implement physically because of the design of suburban sprawl?" The cost and impracticality of most light rail systems proposed in America prevents most of them from ever being implemented. Bullet trains between cities are another matter. However, solving the transportation problem for the sprawling suburbs is a much higher priority.

We can serve the suburbs with a much less expensive Curitiba Style system with a very flexible, mini-bus to transport us to the major bus system, using rubber tire rolling stock, dedicated roadways, and buses fueled by alternative energy, at a fraction of the cost of the dying, petroleum driven, carbon dioxide emitting, car system.

The Curitiba Style BRT will save the commuters thousands of dollars per year. However, we need the President and Congress to fund such systems on a national scale. Otherwise, it is bye, bye, suburbanites, because our system has trapped them, based on the false dream of cheap oil forever. We cannot bull doze millions of homes in the suburbs. We hope this analysis will open some eyes and bring about some rapid action in Congress that has never been seen before in our lifetimes. It means a significant shift from military spending to spending at home to save the livelihoods of millions of suburbanites. This is no exaggeration, simply because the scale of the problem is nationwide. We will also have to bring as many employment centers as possible to the suburbs. Of course, working at home via the Internet is also an option. Yet, what we have constructed to date will require major new transportation systems based on renewable energy.

Satellite New Towns Built Upon Transit Lines

Satellite New Towns can be built within a 25-40 minute Bus Rapid Transit ride to and from major cities. They can be built with multiple purposes: (1) to absorb the increase in population; (2) to provide an affordable transit system within the Satellite New Town and a line to a major city. Here is the key planning feature: the transit lines are built first and then everything else is built with high rises on the transit line: (3) to be built with solar power plants and other alternative energy systems; (4) to be built with plans for local agriculture supply; (5) to be financed by government and private funds, with a return on investment from new commercial development at a few major transit stops. The government would need to use immanent domain to purchase the right-of-way and purchase the land at appropriate and just prices. Eminent Domain could be used because with gas prices rising inexorably, the nation is already in an emergency situation to avoid societal and economic collapse.

In the case of large suburban sprawl, Mini-buses would pick up passengers in the suburbs and take them to and from the Main Line Station. Mini-buses would also be used to take people to their workplace, school or shopping once they arrive in the city and back to the Main Line Station for the trip home.

In order to conserve farm land and local food supply, we need to stop building suburban sprawl and build high rises above the major transit stops. As noted above, the federal government can recoup much of its expenditures for land by selling or leasing land for commercial and other development at the major transit stops. New Town planning and building opens up a wholly new path for human development while combining a new set of the latest technologies, especially in alternative energy production, rapid transit systems, local agricultural systems, and conservation of water and energy. All of these new technologies and economic structures can be put in place in a way that is best for the planet, environmentally wise, and far more affordable for individuals and families within an economic framework that is just and sustainable. Again, it can all be done by purposeful design and determined implementation.

Surely, there are some wise and moral bankers, financiers and industrialists with large amounts of investment capital who are longing to invest in new economic arrangements such as Mondragon Style Satellite New Towns.

If you visit our website, *livelihoodsystems.com*, you will find a video that describes new legislation, pending in Congress, to enable young families to buy a home earlier in life, with tax-free savings at the workplace, which will set up families for a comfortable retirement. Best of all, this plan more than pays for itself from new taxes generated by construction, the housing related industries, the multiplier effect and a reduction in mortgage tax deductions for incomes over $100,000. This video also describes how the Middle Class needs to be re-established by adequate pay and by increasing 401(k) contributions by employers to 7.5% of gross salary as a national standard.

PART 6

SUMMATION

Comprehensive Planning Led by Good Government and Industry

When James Fallows and Jim Rogers, CEO of Duke Energy, saw how fast China was moving they were not just impressed, they were in awe. Then, David Mohler, Duke's chief technology officer, told them: "We learned that China is preparing, by 2025, for 350 million people to live in cities that don't exist now. They have to build the equivalent of the U.S. electrical system – that is, almost as much added capacity as the entire U.S. electrical system –Grid—by 2025. It took us 120 years."[1]

China will be building New Towns on a scale that would house the entire population of the United States in about 15 years. This is "shock and awe" of a dynamically peaceful project – not the "shock and awe" of destruction and warring. Clearly, America needs to turn its full attention to the task of rebuilding America in a totally peaceful demonstration of Christian values. The Chinese are focusing on growth. They are advancing the forward days of humankind by working to solve the problem of what to do with all of that polluting, dirty coal that they perceive (for now) that they must use for energy supplies for a nation of over 1.3 billion people. It is up to America, China and Europe to show the world the forever gift of sun, wind, and renewable power with hydrogen storage as the Final Solution for the providential provisioning of life-giving energy to the world.

The Chinese long range plan to build as much as 350 New Towns is the perfect example of how America needs to scale up, and implement the Nation Builder's Industrial Complex, with renewable electric power. As James Fallows observed in his *Atlantic* article, cited above, "But China's very effectiveness and dynamism, beneficial as that may be in this case, highlight an American failure – a failure that seems not transient or incidental but deep and hard to correct. The deeper problem is the revealed difference in national capacity, in seriousness and ability to deliver. The Chinese government can decide to transform the country's energy system in 10 years, and no one doubts that it will."

A U.S. administration can promise to create a clean-energy revolution, but will our representatives and senators in Congress cooperate? So far, they have not.

"The most impressive aspect of the Chinese performance is their determination to do what is needed," Julio Friedmann told Fallows.

"America obviously is not displaying comparable determination—and the saddest aspect of the U.S. performance is that it seems not deliberate but passive and accidental, the product of modern America's inability to focus public effort on public problems." Clearly, we need to move rapidly beyond short-sightedness and get into national long-range planning with vigor.

There is no value in impugning blame. There is only value in energizing our best and brightest to step forward and deal with the nation's real public problems with a determination and well-planned national effort. This, of course, calls out for leadership at the highest levels. There is no prior example to lead the nation at this scale, even during World War II. Fossil fuels must be phased out after we have used them to create a whole new renewable energy system and a new national electric grid.

It will require many leaders to step up to the challenges ahead, described above. But what a joy! To take on the creative challenge and go up against the future of unaffordable gasoline and oil for the nation!

The "Game Changer" field of international cooperation is wide open and waiting for the next wonderful solution to the fact that oil is now over as a long range future energy source simply because global demand is catching up with available "easy oil" supply, far, far faster than we could have imagined and especially for the United States.

This whole scenario has an immediate impact on the creative human intellect and human will that is unprecedented in our lifetime. We are in the breach and I find it to be a glorious and very positive opportunity for the "advancement of man's forward days," as Bucky Fuller was so fond of encouraging us to do.

When our United States leadership makes an assessment of our nation's challenge to be independent of oil in 30 years, as we hope they are now doing, they will perhaps see that the warring nation of the past must become the most advanced peacemaker in the world. We can now find more constructive jobs for the Military Industrial Complex employees in the Nation Builder's Industrial Complex, and move away from warring.

Obama and the Military Are Leading the Shift to Clean Energy

At a Democratic National Committee fund raiser on April 20, 2011, President Obama began to address rising gasoline prices. Obama said "because we see what's happening in the Middle East and we understand that a finite resource that is primarily located in a very unstable part of the world is not good for our long-term future." This is from an article by Joanna Zelman, "Obama Targets Climate Change Deniers in Congress".[2] He went on to declare that "the U.S. must stop giving $4 billion in taxpayer subsidies to oil companies – instead, the money should be put towards clean energy." Instead of subsidizing yesterday's energy, let's invest in tomorrow's energy. It's good for our security. It will grow the economy, and it will leave our children with a safer and cleaner planet. We must invest in clean energy, he said, mentioning solar and wind power as well as hydrogen/electric cars. Ms. Zelman's article notes that in a speech, President Obama acknowledged that change will not happen overnight, but that he aims to reduce oil imports by one-third by 2025. At the same time, the Navy and the Air Force plan to fly their aircraft on a 50%/50% blend of kerosene and biofuels and they have put out the call to biofuel producers to "bring it on".

The shift from warring to producing clean energy has begun. The House of Representatives, which controls the budget, needs to move more aggressively in the right direction to give the U.S. "national security" at home. Delay is no longer an option because the timeframe requires action here and now and for decades to come.

The world needs an economic system with Christ's values of Truth, Goodness, and Justice and pursuit of the common good. Economic competition drags wages down, as the record shows. As Pope Francis wrote in his *Joy of the Gospel*, "unfettered capitalism" has created "a new tyranny" and "such is an economy that kills."

The primary function of a good and true economic system is to provide working families with "livelihood systems", i.e., decent paying jobs, an affordable home, financial security, education for our children, health care and a comfortable retirement, in exchange for a lifetime of work.

To undertake Nation Building at Home, we need to develop and establish regional alliances between worker-owned cooperatives. We need to establish regional Mondragon-Style cooperative banks and place our retirement savings in those banks in order to create more sustainable livelihoods, and employment for all. We need to move most of our money out of Wall Street and invest it in our own Mondragon style banks, which can invest in livelihood systems for all of us.

A New Growth Model Based on Mondragon Cooperatives

Existing enlightened corporations may wisely choose to transform themselves into Mondragon-Style cooperatives. This is especially good for the small and medium sized businesses of America, which comprise 50% of the economy and create 80% of new jobs, according to the Department of Labor. However, a huge number of small businesses fail due to lack of bank loans to sustain them. The Mondragon style banking system is a giant step toward keeping small businesses alive and millions of workers employed.

Small and medium sized businesses need to band together, regionally, and establish Mondragon style banks to have working capital; advance trade among them and give each other a way to advance their own business and the forward days of humankind.

In order to create enough employment for people, we need to create more energy from the Sun and wind and let that energy do most of the work by driving machines that make machines and assembly lines that do the work. This will require new worker-owned cooperative corporations and their new business model for the redistribution of wealth that they can deliver to workers. *Growth then would come from the creation and redistribution of energy.* Planners would need to decrease the amount of the world's resources used by humanity. This can be done by building solar and wind power facilities nationally and globally. Once these facilities are built the sun and the wind are free! Agricultural practices must protect and create new topsoil to re-establish a sustainable loop of food production which would require the employment of a larger percentage of the population. We have all of the technology to accomplish these things. What is needed is a shift from the old and dying greedy business model to the cooperative business model. Rather than encouraging greed at the top and the worship of money we can shift to a cooperative, sharing attitude in the culture in order to survive.

The cost of gasoline at the pump is out of American control. Oil prices are now determined internationally because the demand for oil is global. China, India and Asia are consuming more oil and raising prices. Producing more oil in the U.S. will *not bring down gasoline prices at the pump* because we can't produce enough to bring prices down globally and we have to import huge amounts of oil until we can replace it with renewable energy, hydrogen/electric cars and bus rapid transit systems.

American corporations have gone abroad to make higher profits and they have created oil consuming middle classes in foreign countries. Rather than focusing on nation building at home, ironically, they are driving up gasoline prices around the globe.

As noted above, U.S. military long-range planners have reported that America cannot guarantee the *affordability or availability* of oil and gasoline at prices that are affordable by 2040. This is, of course, true for the domestic economy and we need to shift from oil to renewable energy and hydrogen/electric cars. Domestic airlines may only be viable with an enormous upscaling of biofuels. Reinvesting in the entire transportation system is now a pressing national priority and it requires aggressive long range planning and implementation.

Climate change is now causing disastrous tornados, hurricanes, wild fires from drought and unheard of floods around the globe, forcing millions of people out of their homes. The United Nations Intergovernmental Panel on Climate Change (IPCC) scientists have shown that the world must not generate more than 450 parts per million of carbon dioxide or we face disasters that may be irreversible, for centuries. We have already reached CO_2 emissions of 400 parts per million. The need to shift from fossil fuels to renewable energy is now at a lethal threat level. We are at "Defcon 10".

As noted above, the critical tipping point is the release of massive amounts of methane from the 9 million square kilometers of permafrost all across the northern hemisphere.

If that happens, as Professor Douglas McPherson remarked, "Stick a fork in us, we're done." We cannot allow that to happen.

Those politicians, who deny the findings of the IPCC with 2,000 scientists from 154 countries, need to simply get off the public stage and hide themselves from public view, for they are now a laughing stock, not deserving of another year in office. The world must move rapidly to meet these challenges with a much higher priority than warring and empire building ever merited because now we are faced with human survival in the U.S. and around the globe.

In order to meet these challenges, trillions of dollars over the coming years must be shifted from warring and empire building to nation building at home. Former Defense Secretary Gates has blasted wars like those in Iraq and Afghanistan as huge mistakes, never to be repeated again. The Department of Defense (DOD) is pursuing the task of developing solar energy and biofuels to replace oil in all of their aircraft and vehicles within the next 30 years. The DOD is rapidly installing wind and solar power on U.S. military bases.

Solar Thermal Power Plants, wind and hydrogen storage can now replace most of America's 300 coal-fired and natural gas power plants. The technology is well proven and the production cost for solar thermal and wind power are now the lowest cost energy sources—they are no longer "alternative energies", as declared by *The Economist* magazine. When natural gas energy plants are constructed they must continually be fed with fuel from drilling. Clearly, solar and wind power are by far the lowest cost energy sources when the awesome cost of not addressing global warming is taken into account. The wind blows somewhere all of the time. We need an electric grid that can supply power plants at all times. It logically follows that investors will rush to produce solar and wind power energy, once the Crony Capitalists who control Congress are dismissed in favor saving the nation from death by fossil fuels.

Why Barreling Down the Road with "Fracking" Natural Gas Is Deadly

Natural gas production, on a large scale, cannot be a long term bridge until we produce renewable energy because it generates too much carbon dioxide, which we can no longer afford to add to the greenhouse heating effect. As cited above, by Michael Strahan, natural gas is NOT clean energy as advertised. *Natural gas burning releases only about 11% less carbon dioxide into the biosphere than oil!* Now, that is a big wake up call for a nation that has been brain-washed, through TV advertising, by the natural gas fracking companies. Hydraulic Fracturing, or "Fracking" leaks large amounts of methane, which is 20 times more deadly than releasing carbon dioxide into the atmosphere. Can we allow corporations to destroy the human species for their "deified" market profits? As Pope Francis wrote in *Joy of the Gospel:* "No to the idolatry of money."

We must move directly to renewable energy, just as the German engineers have decided for the European Union by adopting the Third Industrial Revolution path developed by Jeremy Rifkin.[2] America can follow that path by establishing it on a regional basis that interlocks over the entire continent.

America Needs a National Renewable Energy Plan without Delay

America needs a National Renewable Energy Plan and a National Transportation Plan in order to meet the future without too expensive gasoline and to address global warming. The Institute of Physics published a report on February 16, 2012, claiming that the rapid deployment of low-greenhouse-gas-emitting technologies will initially *increase* emissions because they will require a large amount of energy to construct and install. The report stated: "Delaying the rollout of the technologies is not an option, however; the risks of environmental harm will be much greater in the second half of the century and beyond if we continue to rely on coal-based technologies."[3]

Satellite New Towns Built on Rapid Transit Systems Must Replace Urban Sprawl

America's vast urban sprawl needs an overhaul. This can be accomplished by providing electric/hydrogen mini buses for passenger pick-up at stations one quarter mile from each house. The mini buses can take passengers to a Bus Rapid

Transit Station, which can transport people to central locations, with mini buses available to transport them to their jobs in central cities and within their neighborhoods. This will enable suburban one car families to reach employment sites, day-care, shopping and entertainment.

New urban sprawl must be stopped. Instead, Satellite New Towns need to be developed for an expanding population by being built vertically (high rises) on top of transportation systems. Satellite New Towns with renewable energy, sustainable food production and cooperative workplaces can transform our lives and solve several interlocking problems by design. Satellite new towns must be built vertically above Bus Rapid Transit Lines from the onset, with flexible rubber tire rolling stock, on dedicated roadways. Also, work centers need to be built in suburbia so that people can get to their office by bicycle or walking.

Infinite Solar/Wind with Hydrogen Storage Needs to Replace Finite Oil

Thousands of scientists and engineers have reached the conclusion that harvesting the Sun's radiation and wind power are the best and safest way to supply energy to the world, as a near eternal source. As huge numbers of scientists continue to focus their skills on this task, I predict that the results will continue to be astonishing. The world will learn to love the sunshine and wind in a totally new way as it can dramatically reduce our labors, provide the basic necessities more easily and drive machines that make machines and assembly lines. Hydrogen provides a storage system when electricity is used to create hydrogen and then, when the sun doesn't shine and the wind doesn't blow, hydrogen can be converted back into electricity. It is expensive now but it eliminates carbon dioxide emissions. The emissions of CO_2 and methane are far more costly and destructive than most people can imagine as they continue to raise the temperature of the Planet Earth, which can eventually destroy all sea life and then, all human life.

Economic Systems Need To Provide Sustainable Livelihood Systems, Globally

There are over 50 million unemployed or underemployed young people in the Middle East and North Africa. The World Economic Forum has determined that 40% of youth are unemployed worldwide. However, they are protesting against government leaders when they should be protesting against corporate and banking leaders who actually control the entire economic system.

The revolutions of the "Arab Spring" sweeping the Middle East and the destructive austerity economic attempts in Europe, and now in the United States can no longer be ignored. All of this requires a sustainable job creation system for working families and for millions of young people who rightfully demand to have a life. Sustainable job creation with sustainable livelihoods is the basic foundation of any economic system worth its salt. How could it be otherwise? Economists have "deified" the "market" as if it is infallible, and "this is an economy that kills" as Pope Francis wrote. "Creative destruction" of jobs in order to advance unsustainable growth and profit for a few is not an option now. That is an economist's mistake that we must move beyond. Dynamic research and technological improvement is good and necessary, however, it must be done in a way that creates jobs for people. The Mondragon Cooperative Corporation has shown that it can be done within an organization that cares about people with their business and banking model.

Corporate Responsibility to Employees

All corporations should follow Mondragon's lead by using long range planning to avoid massive layoffs, through retraining, education and transfers to new jobs internally or to cooperating corporations. "Creative destruction" is really "uncreative destruction of livelihoods" through managerial malfeasance and the uncaring lack of positive planning and action. Firing 10,000 people at a time is a criminal act, because it takes away people's very livelihoods! How can such a destructive act be legal? Corporations need to be proactive in providing livelihoods. Surprise! People's livelihoods come before profits. Mondragon has shown how that can be done even in a globally competitive economy. What a concept!

Retirement plans have been underfunded, systematically plundered and eliminated almost entirely at the will of corporations. Corporations should be required to contribute a minimum of 7.5% of gross salary to 401(k) plans instead of the paltry 3% median that they contribute now. This will encourage employees to contribute 7.5% as well, which can result in a sufficient retirement income along with Social Security. However, people need to know that if they see a bubble collapse coming, or in progress, they can shift their 401(k) money out of the stock market into a cash account, in order to avoid losing more than 10%-40% of their life's savings. This shift to cash can be done without a capital gains taxation penalty! Check it out. When you know that you can shift your 401(k) money to cash, with no penalty, it could save you from destitution.

The priority is to take loving care of the people in every nation, which is true, people-serving economics and those who oppose it must be confronted and shown that they are denying empathy, truth, goodness and justice, as taught by Christ. This is not socialism or Marxist—these are Christ's teachings!

Sustainable Development with a New Growth Model

America can lead the way by building a nation of regional cooperatives which invest the retirement savings of their own employees back into the cooperative enterprise, creating sustainable jobs. The old economic growth model needs to be replaced by a model that lets the sun, wind and hydrogen do the work, with a lateral distributive electric grid, as described by Jeremy Rifkin in *The Third Industrial Revolution*. Then cooperatives can distribute the wealth gained back to the workers who created that wealth with their investment and their labor. Sustainable development would then be based on renewable energy, lateral distribution and sharing of the energy and wealth created. Growth in wealth then would no longer be based on outsourcing jobs to areas of extremely low wages. Growth in wealth would no longer require such a large amount of depletion of natural resources. The economy can grow at the rate that we shift to renewable energies, letting Sun, wind and geothermal energy drive machines and processes that replace human labor. The productivity gain from renewable energy, Information technology and computers *must be distributed as wealth to all levels of the population.*

The bell-shaped curve of intelligence shows that 50% of the population is above average (100 points on the test) and 50% of the population is below 100 points. Today, 47 million people live in U.S. households that are below the poverty line. The "free enterprise system" does not create enough decent-paying jobs for the top 50%, yet alone for the bottom 50%. Furthermore, the current economic system does not distribute wealth in a just and caring manner. That is why Middle Class taxpayers are asked to pay for the safety net for the poor and this is what infuriates the Tea Party! If most of the people in the lower 50%

of the Intelligence quotient were provided with the dignity of a decent paying job, the Middle Class would not have to pay so much in taxes to support that safety net to keep people from starvation. Corporate control has shifted wealth, for over three decades, from the 99% to the top 0.1%. Clearly, we can reduce "Big Government" taxation by distributing the wealth we create in a more just and productive manner—back to We the People. The wealth we create and resulting taxes can no longer go to the Military Industrial Complex in such large measure, but must be shifted to productive work that benefits the nation.

The "Driving Forces" of the need for sustainable livelihoods, renewable energy and a zero carbon economy are interconnected and so is their solution through nation building at home. To accomplish this task we must undertake Long Range National and Regional Plans for Energy, Transportation and Sustainable Livelihoods. We can no longer back into the future taking baby steps as we sleep walk.

Delay Is Not an Option

The mobilization of the nations will require honest reflection and honest reporting by the mainstream media, the governments around the world, the world-wide corporate leaders, the pope, the major financial institutions, major investors, OPEC, China, India, Brazil, South America, and all of the leaders of Islam and Israel. It will also require fast moving CHANGE! Delay in implementation of a Global Energy and Transportation

Plan is the greatest threat to American citizens and the entire global economy. The pace of this change must be dramatically accelerated in order to prevent the panic situation that politicians rightly fear the most. The Third Industrial Revolution path, authored by Jeremy Rifkin, is an excellent model. It replaces the old top down, centralized authoritarian model with a new distributed, collaborative model which gives power and wealth to the people who create that energy wealth. With the Mondragon Cooperative Corporation system, we have a business model and a banking model that work to serve humankind rather than to rule over us.

Discovering Our True Selves in the Last Days

In order to arrive at a society that distributes the wealth we create, we will need to overcome our selfish egos. We will need to find our true selves and leave the false self behind. As Albert Nolan wrote in *Jesus Today*:

"Jesus image for your true self is your clear eye, your eye without a log or any other obstruction. 'Take the log out of your own eye, and then you will see clearly' (Luke 6:42) 'Your eye is the lamp of your body. If your eye is healthy, your whole body is full of light; but if it is not healthy, your body is full of darkness.' (Luke 11:34) Your true self is buried below your ego or false self, below the log of wood."

Some people refer to the selfish ego as "human nature" and they say that you will never change "human nature." However, that is exactly what Jesus came down to Earth to accomplish. He came to show our hearts that God loves us. We can not only think that God loves us but we can *feel* that God loves us and everyone else. Once we know and feel that God loves us we can overcome the selfish ego and share with one another, as they do in a worker/owner cooperative economic structure. You may ask how can people have a spiritual transformation and overcome their selfish egos? The answer comes from an old prophesy by Joel, quoted by Peter in the Book of Acts:

"In the last days I will pour out my spirit upon all flesh, and your sons and daughters shall prophesy and your young men shall see visions and your old men shall dream dreams." God can do anything He wants. Mankind may find it impossible "to change human nature", but because God loves us all, He can pour out his Holy Spirit upon us and we can be made whole, and feel our oneness with God, all people and the whole universe.

This can be the dawning of peace on the planet and the end of warring as we provide peoples on the planet with what they need to survive, thrive and grow in compassion for one another. Christ's final loving encouragement, "As I have loved you, so also must you love one another," (John 13:35) can now be implemented.

NOTES

Introduction

1. Pope Francis, Joy of the Gospel, Vatican.va, 2013, Chapter 2.
2. Ibid.
3. Jeremy Rifkin, *The End of Work,* Penguin Group, New York, 1995 and 2004, p. 288.
4. Robert Kunzig, "World Without Ice", National Geographic, October 2011, p. 90.
5. Pope Francis, The Joy of the Gospel, Vatican.va, 2013, Chapter 2.
6. Albert Nolan, *Jesus Today*: A Spirituality of Radical Freedom, Orbis Books, 2006, p. 164.
7. Robert Bellah, et all, *Habits of the Heart: Individualism and Commitment in American Life,* Berkeley, CA: University of California Press, 1985.
8. David C. Korten, *The Great Turning, From Empire to Earth Community*, People –Centered Development Forum 2006, co-published by Kumarian Press, Inc. and Berrett-Koehler Publishers, Inc.
9. Buckminster Fuller, *Operating Manual for the Spaceship Earth*, University of Southern Illinois Press, 1969.

PART 1
A NEW WAY OF DOING BUSINESS WITH COOPERATION: WORKER OWNED WORKPLACES

1. Pope Francis, *Joy of the Gospel,* Vatican.va, 2013, Chapter 2.
2. Roy Morrison, *We Build the Road as We Travel,* New Society Publishers, 1991, pages 11-12.
3. Ibid.
4. Ibid.

5. Greg McCloud, "From Mondragon to America", University College of Breton Press, February 2, 1998.
6. Albert Nolan, *Jesus Today,* Orbis Books, 2006.
7. Stephen C. Meyer, The Signature in the Cell: DNA and the Evidence for Intelligent Design, Harper Collins, 2009.
8. James Miller, *Living Systems,* New York, McGraw Hill, 1978.
9. Albert Nolan, *Jesus Today:* A Spirituality of Radical Freedom, Orbis Books, 2006, p. 174.
10. Ibid, p. 173
11. Ibid, p. 175
12. Ibid.
13. Roy Morrison, *We Build the Road as We Travel,* New Society Publishers, Philadelphia, 1991, p. 16.
14. *The Economist* staff, Germany's banking system, Old-fashioned but in favor, The Economist, November 10, 2012, p. 77.
15. Albert Nolan, *Jesus Today,* Orbis Books, 2006.
16. Ibid.
17. Roy Morrison, *We Build the Road as We Travel,* New Society Publishers, Philadelphia, 1991.
18. Ibid.
19. E. J. Dionne, Jr., *The Washington Post,* 1973.
20. Roy Morrison, *We Build the Road as We Travel,* p. 28.
21. Oxfam Briefing Paper 178, "Working for the Few", January 20, 2014.

PART 2
THE OIL CRUNCH IS GUARANTEED

1. U.S. Joint Forces Command, "The Joint Operating Environment", March 15, 2010.
2. Christine Pathemore and John Nagl, "Fueling the Future Force", Center for a New American Security, 2004.
3. Ibid.

4. Ibid.
5. David Pitt, The Palm Beach Post, "International markets diversify your 401(k) January 22, 2011 p. 10B.
6. Peter H. Diamandis and Steve Kotler, *Abundance: The Future Is Better than You Think,* Free Press, New York, 2012, p. 163.
7. Ibid.
8. Ibid.
9. The Economist, "Briefing: The Future of Biofuels", October 30, 2010, p.84
10. Jeremy Rifkin, *The Third Industrial Revolution*, palgrave Mcmillan, 2011, p. 17.
11. Ibid.
12. Michael T. Klare, "A Tough-Oil World", Huffington Post, 3-13-2012.
13. Paul Gilding, *The Great Disruption: Why Climate Change Will Bring an End of Shopping and the Birth of a New World.*
14. Alex Kuhlman, "Peak oil and the collapse of commercial aviation", AIRWAYS, 2006.

PART 3
SOLUTIONS: GERMANY LEADS THE WAY TO ELIMINATE CO2 AND BUILD A NEW GLOBAL ECONOMY

1. Jeremy Rifkin, "Beyond the Financial Crisis: Germany's Plan to Regrow the Global Economy", www. Huffingtonpost.com, 10/24/2011.
2. Ibid.
3. Ibid.
4. Ibid.
5. Jeremy Rifkin, *The Third Industrial Revolution*, palgrave Mcmillan, 2011, p.45.
6. Ibid, p. 36

7. Jeremy Rifkin, "Beyond the Financial Crisis: Germany's Plan to Regrow the Global Economy", www. Huffingtonpost.com, 10/24/2011.

8. Jeremy Rifkin, *The Third Industrial Revolution*, palgrave Mcmillan, 2011, p. 59

9. Ibid, p. 144.

10. Brendan Smith and Jeremy Brecher, "The Rise of the Power Co-op Movement," Common Dreams.org article.

11. Jeremy Rifkin, "Beyond the Financial Crisis: Germany's Plan to Regrow the Global Economy", www. Huffingtonpost.com, 10/24/2011.

12. Ibid.

13. Tudor Vieru, New Method to Extract Hydrogen from Seawater, www. Softpedia.com/news, 10/31/2011.

14. Mark Z. Jacobson, Cristina L. Archer, "Saturation wind power potential and its implications for wind energy", *Proceedings of the National Academy of Sciences*, 2012, DOI:10.1073/pnas. 1208993109

15. David Fogarty, "World's Largest Investors Call for Climate Change Action", Reuters/Posted 11/20/2012, The Huffington Post.com, 2012/11/20.

16. Geoffrey B. Holland and James J. Provenzano, *The Hydrogen Age*, Empowering a Clean-Energy Future, Gibbs Smith, publisher, 2007, p. 17.

17. Vanessa Ko, "Hydrogen fuel-cell cars look to overtake electric autos," for CNN, CNN.com, 11/26/2012.

18. Buckminster Fuller, *Operating Manual for the Spaceship Earth,* Southern Illinois University Press, 1969.

19. *The Economist,* "The Other Kind of Solar Power", June 6, 2009.

20. Vivian Norris, "Here Comes the Sun: Tunisia to Energize Europe", Huffington Post, 1/28/2012.

21. Peter Diamondis and Steven Kotler, *Abundance: The Future Is Better than You Think,* Free Press, New York, New York, 2012, p. 169.

22. Lester Brown, "Getting the Market to tell Ecological Truths", Inter Press Service, April 11, 2012, as reported on commondreams.org.

23. David Strahan, "The great gas showdown", New Scientist, February 25, 2012.

24. Ibid.

25. Strauss, Benjamin, "Rapid accumulation of committed sea-level rise from global warming," Proceedings of the National Academy of Sciences, 2013. Google Benjamin Strauss.

26. Nick Collins, "Oceans acidifying at 'unparalleled' rate", opednews.com, March 3, 2012.

27. Frank Sheed, *Theology and Sanity,* Ignatius Press, San Francisco, original 1947, republished in 1993.

28. Allen F. Matthews, "Humanity's Precious Grubstake" Christian Science Monitor, October 19, 1979.

29. Jared Bernstein, "U.S. Manufacturing Competiveness in Global Trade", published in the Huffington Post, 12-28-2011.

PART 4
SHIFTING MONEY FROM THE MILITARY TO NATION BUILDING AT HOME

1. Robert Gates, "Blasts wars like Iraq, Afghanistan", *The Palm Beach Post*, February 26, 2011, p. 2A

2. Christopher Hellman, "The Real National Security Budget: the Figure No One Wants You To See", website: TomDispatch. com, March 2, 2011.

3. Miriam Pemberton, "Military Spending is the Weakest Job Creator", *Foreign Policy in Focus,* December 13, 2011.

4. Richard J. Barnet, "REFLECTIONS After the Cold War", The New Yorker, January 1, 1990.

5. KurzweilAI/Accelerating Intelligence. News, April 11, 2014. "Navy researchers demonstrate flight powered by fuel created from seawater."

6. Common Dreams staff, "Meteorologists Adjust Official Stance: Human Activity Causing Climate Change.

7. James Fallows, *The Atlantic*, "Dirty Coal Clean Energy", December 2010.

8. Steve Connor, "Shock as Retreat of Arctic Sea Ice Releases Deadly Greenhouse Gas", *The Independent/UK*, December 14, 2011.

9. Ibid.

10. Fionna Harvey, "Renewable Energy Can Power the World, Says Landmark IPCC Study", The Guardian/UK, May 9, 2011.

11. The Associated Press, "Obama urges shift to new energy sources", The Palm Beach Post, March 8, 2012, p. 2A.

12. Justin Gills and Kenneth Chang, "Experts: Antarctic ice collapse started", New York Times, May 13,2014.

13. Robert Kunzig, "WORLD WITHOUT ICE", National Geographic, October 2011, p. 90.

14. Common Dreams staff, Common Dreams.org, "Costs of Climate Change Touching Down All Around: Insurers Confirm Growing Risks, Costs", March 3, 2012.

PART 5
NEW TOWN BUILDING AND SUSTAINABLE LIVELIHOOD SYSTEMS

1. Jeremy Rifkin, *The End of Work*, Penguin Group, New York, 1995 and 2004.

2. Joseph Goodman, Melissa Laube and Judith Schwenk, "Curitiba's Bus System is Model for Rapid Transit", Urban Habitat, December 16, 2010, p. 4.

PART 6
SUMMATION

1. James Fallows, The Atlantic, "Dirty Coal, Clean Future", December 2010, p. 7
2. Zelman, Joanna, "Obama Targets Climate Change Deniers in Congress", posted on The Huffington Post, April 21, 2011.
3. Myhrvold M.P. and Caldeira K., "Greenhouse gases, climate change and the transition from coal to low-carbon technologies, *Environmental Research Letters*, February 16, 2012. This paper can be downloaded from http://iopscience.iop.org.

BIBLIOGRAPHY

1. Barnet, Richard J., "REFLECTIONS: After the Cold War", New Yorker, January 1, 1990.

2. Bellah, Robert et al, Habits of the Heart: Individualism and Commitment in American Life, Berkeley, CA, University of California Press, 1985.

3. Broecker, Wallace S. and Robert Kunzig, *Fixing Climate*, Hill and Wang, New York, 2008.

4. Brown, Lester, "Getting the Market to Tell Ecological Truths", Inter Press Service, April 11, 2012.

5. Conneta, Carl, "The Pentagon's Runaway Budget", Project on Defense Spending, website: antiwar.com.

6. Connor, Steve, "Shock as Retreat of Arctic Sea Ice Releases Deadly Greenhouse Gas," *The Independent/UK*, December 14, 2011.

7. Cooke, Sonia Van Gilder, New Scientist, "Salty Solar Power Plant Store's Sun's Heat", December 11, 2010.

8. Davidson, Carl, "Steelworkers Aim at Job Creation with Worker-Owned Factories", website: www.SolidarityEconomiy.net.

9. Diamondis, Peter and Steven Kotler, *Abundance: The Future Is Better than You Think*, Free Press, New York, New York, 2012, p. 126.

10. E. J. Dionne, Jr., *The Washington Post*, 1973.

11. Ecofys, "The Energy Report", (a leading energy consulting firm in the Netherlands, 2011.

12. *The Economist,* multiple entries. (See chapter notes.)

13. Fallows, James, The Atlantic, "Dirty Coal Clean Future", December 2010.

14. Fuller, Buckminster, *Operating Manual for the Spaceship Earth*, Southern Illinois University Press, March 1969.

15. Gates, Robert, "Blasts Wars Like Iraq and Afghanistan", The Palm Beach Post, February 26, 2011.

16. Gilding, Paul, *The Great Disruption: Why Climate Change Will Bring an End of Shopping and the Birth of a New World.*

17. Gills, Justin and Kenneth Chang, "Experts: Antarctic ice collapse started", The New York Times, May 13, 2014.

18. Goodman, Joseph, Melissa Laube and Judith Schwenk, "Curitiba's Bus System is Model for Rapid Transit, "Urban Habitat", December 16, 2010.

19. Harvey, Fiona, "Renewable Energy Can Power the World Says Landmark IPCC Study, The Guardian/UK, May 9, 2011.

20. Hellman, Christopher, "The Real National Security Budget: the Figure No One Wants You to See", website, TomDispatch.com, March 2, 2011.

21. Holland, Geoffrey B. and James J. Provenzano, *The Hydrogen Age,* Gibbs Smith, publisher, 2007.

22. Klare, Michael T., *The Race for What's Left: The Global Scramble for the World's Last Resources*, Metropolitan Books, 2012.

23. Ko, Vanessa, "Hydrogen fuel cell cars look to overtake electric autos," for CNN.com, 11/26/2012.

24. Korten, David C. *The Great Turning- From Empire to Earth Community,* People-Centered Development Forum, 2006.

25. Kuhlman, Alex, "Peak oil and the collapse of commercial aviation", AIRWAYS, 2006.

26. Kunzig, Robert, "World Without Ice", National Geographic, October, 2011. p. 90.

27. KurzweilAI, Accelerating Intelligence, News, "Cracking cellulose: a step into the biofuels future", September 2,2011.

28. Lee, Mara, "Toll from Weather Disasters in US This Year Hits $52 Billion, *Hartford Courant,* December 8, 2011.

29. Louda, William Professor of Environmental Chemistry at Florida Atlantic University.

30. Maslow, Abraham H., *The Farther Reaches of Human Nature,* Viking Press, New York, 1971, by Bertha G. Maslow.

31. McCloud, Gregg, "From Mondragon to America", University College of Breton Press, February 2,1998. Also, "The Mondragon Experiment, The Public Purpose Corporation", Harvard International Review, April 4, 2009.

32. Morrison, Roy, *We Build the Road as We Travel,* New Society Publishers, Philadelphia, 1991.

33. Matthews, Allen F., "Humanity's Precious Grubstake", Christian Science Monitor, October 19, 1979.

34. Nolan, Albert, *Jesus Today, A Spirituality of Radical Freedom,* Orbis Books, Maryknoll, New York, 2006.

35. Norris, Vivian, "Here Comes the Sun: Tunisia to Energize Europe", The Huffington Post, 1/28/2012.

36. Parthemore, Christine and John Nagl, "Fueling the Future Force", Center for a New American Security, Washington, D.C., September 2004.

37. Pemberton, Miriam, "Military Spending is the Weakest Job Creator," *Foreign Policy in Focus*, December 13, 2011.

38. Pitt, David, "International markets diversify your 401(k), The Palm Beach Post, January 22, 2011.

39. Rifkin, Jeremy, *The Third Industrial Revolution,* palgrave McMillan, 2011. Also, "Beyond the Financial Crisis: Germany's Plan to Regrow the Global Economy, www. Huffington post.com 10/24/2011.

40. Rifkin, Jeremy, *The End of Work,* Penguin Group, New York, 1995 and 2004.

41. Salsbury, Susan, "FPL's solar stars shine at new 500-acre array", The Palm Beach Post, March 5, 2011, p. 6B.

42. Science Magazine, "Scaling Up Alternative Energy", August 13, 2010, p. 782.

43. Sheed, Frank, *Theology and Sanity,* Ignatius Press, San Francisco, 1946, 1993.

44. Strahan, David, "The great gas showdown", New Scientist, February 25, 2012 p.48.

45. Strauss, Benjamin, "Rapid accumulation of committed sea-level rise from global warming", *Proceedings of the National Academy of Sciences*, 2013. Google: Benjamin Strauss.

46. United Steel Workers News, Report, January 5, 2011. Zelman, Joanna, "Obama Targets Climate Change Deniers in Congress", posted on The Huffington Post, April 21, 2011.